The
Path
Within

TALKS BY TEACHERS OF THE
DHARMA REALM BUDDHIST ASSOCIATION

REVEREND HENG SURE | BHIKSHU HENG LAI
BHIKSHU HENG LYU | BHIKSHUNI HENG CHIH
MARTIN VERHOEVEN | DOUG POWERS

Published by Buddhist Text Translation Society,
Ukiah, California

The Path Within: Talks by Teachers of the Dharma Realm Buddhist Association

Buddhist Text Translation Society
Attn: Permissions Coordinator
4951 Bodhi Way, Ukiah, CA 95482
www.buddhisttexts.org | info@buddhisttexts.org

First edition 2024

ISBN 978-1-64217-150-1 paperback | ISBN 978-1-64217-151-8 ebook

Library of Congress Cataloging-in-Publication Data

Names: Buddhist Text Translation Society, compiler. |
Dharma Realm Buddhist Association, issuing body.

Title: The path within : talks by teachers of the Dharma Realm Buddhist Association /
as spoken by: Reverend Heng Sure, Bhikshu Heng Lai, Bhikshu Heng Lyu, Bhikshuni
Heng Chih, Martin Verhoeven, Doug Powers.

Description: 1st edition. | Ukiah : Buddhist Text Translation Society, 2024. | Summary:
"This anthology of talks by teachers in the Dharma Realm Buddhist Association presents
Buddhist teachings practically. It not only includes teachings on the four noble truths and
meditation, but also on devotional practices such as recitation and bowing-and even on
spending the holidays with family. The book is accessible for beginners and informative
also for long-term practitioners"-- Provided by publisher.

Identifiers: LCCN 2024006557 (print) | LCCN 2024006558 (ebook) | ISBN
9781642171501 (paperback) | ISBN 9781642171518 (ebook)

Subjects: LCSH: Spiritual life--Zen Buddhism. | Zen Buddhism--Doctrines. |
Meditation--Buddhism.

Classification: LCC BQ9288 .P38 2024 (print) | LCC BQ9288 (ebook) |
DDC 294.3/44--dc23/eng/20240328

LC record available at https://lccn.loc.gov/2024006557
LC ebook record available at https://lccn.loc.gov/2024006558

Contents

Editorial Introduction

After an evening class co-taught by Dharma Master Heng Chih and Doug Powers, a few of us were walking back to our dorms. We were inspired. We were feeling really fortunate and very blessed to have the opportunity to learn from such great teachers. As young Dharma practitioners, the chance to learn from long-term practitioners is valuable in and of itself. But what makes these teachers especially precious to us is that they speak our language and share our culture. Learning from them brings Buddhism to life in our lives: it is not a foreign, exotic tradition. Rather, its practices and principles can guide us in our own paths to great compassion and true freedom.

The conversation on the way back to our dorms however was not about this inspiration. No. We were reflecting on how few of us have the chance to learn from these teachers. The Dharma — Sanskrit for "truth" or "teaching" — has enriched our lives a tremendous amount and we could see no greater joy than to share it with others. The question that evening was: But how?

That late night conversation happened a number of years ago and an attempt at an answer now lies in your hands. In this collection you find excerpts from lectures by some of the senior teachers in the Dharma Realm Buddhist Association who never fail to inspire us. We hope they will inspire you as well.

We have selected the talks for accessibility and practicality. Our hope is that this book can be an entryway for those new to Buddhism and can serve as a guide in the practice of Buddhism. That said, we cannot promise the complete beginner that everything will be crystal-clear. Our advice is that if something does go over your head, just focus on the parts you understand. Over time, when your practice and understanding have grown, and you then revisit puzzling paragraphs, you will find the pieces falling into place naturally.

In a similar vein, we hope this selection will also serve more advanced practitioners. The talks in this collection offer varying degrees of depth that may not be fathomed in one reading. We encourage you to consider how these perspectives of other practitioners might enhance your own experiences. Perhaps a familiar concept will be illuminated in a new way; perhaps a principle never understood will suddenly click unexpectedly; or perhaps you will be brought back to the simplicity of practice.

The talks in this collection are quite varied. There is no overarching theme—apart from, obviously, the application of the Buddha's teachings. It is up to you in which order you read them. Nevertheless, we have put some thought into the presentation of the talks and ordered them in a way that starts with more conceptual talks and moves toward the practical, offering beginners a solid place to start and sharing insights that may resonate with seasoned practitioners.

We hope this collection will aid you in your journey; that it will nourish the growth of your wisdom and compassion; and that it will ultimately bring you back to your true home.

Acknowledgments

Since that first conversation, many people have been involved with this project. It has been wonderful to work together as Dharma friends. The list of contributors is too long. But we hope it will be clear: thank you all! We give special thanks to Meina Co for her excellent work on the design of the book and the cover.

We could never know how to thank Reverend Heng Sure, Dharma Master Lai, Dharma Master Lyu, Dharma Master Chih, Doug Powers, and Martin Verhoeven—for practicing the Dharma all those years, for sharing your wisdom, and for encouraging our growth. And along with our teachers, we share a profound sense of gratitude to the Venerable Master Hsuan Hua, who has been essential in bringing Dharma to the West.

The Editorial Team

The Bodhi Resolve

Reverend Heng Sure

An excerpt from Rev. Heng Sure's weekly lecture on the Avataṃsaka Sūtra at the Berkeley Buddhist Monastery, September 29, 2012.

Bodhisattvas are awakened beings. They are humans who are altruistic, who have good hearts, who are kind and selfless. They are the kind of people who help others before they help themselves. In their minds, helping others is helping themselves, there is no difference.

The Bodhisattva in our text, the *Avataṃsaka Sūtra*, is in training—he or she, it doesn't matter—

on the Third Ground, on the third of ten stages.[1] At this stage, he or she has been watching living beings going through all kinds of unhappiness. Further, he has been reducing the barriers between himself and others. He doesn't stop with his skin. He is very much tuned in to others and he sees how confused they can be.

The *Avataṃsaka Sūtra* is taking us through his progressive awakening. Step by step he realized that things are moving, things are transient, the material things of the world and also states of mind are in flux, they are constantly moving and changing. He also noticed that when we hold onto things, when we grab them, especially the ones we like, and then they go into flux—they move and change—that it's painful. It hurts when things break up, when things go bad, when things age, when they vanish. So he wants to wake people up to that reality, to the real nature of all conditioned things.

So he sets himself the challenge of learning how to wake people up to that reality. His answer is the Buddhadharma.[2] He thinks, "The Dharma is the way.

[1.] There are Ten Grounds or Stages on the path of a Bodhisattva working towards Buddhahood. The third ground is the Ground of Emitting Light.

[2.] The teachings or methods of practice (Dharma) taught by the Buddha.

I want people to learn the Dharma because then they won't be quite so stuck when things change. They'll be able to roll with it. They'll be able to take the bumps on the road and adapt and respond and let go as necessary when things change." So that's where we are now: where the Bodhisattva says, "Right... Buddhadharma! That's what I want. How do I learn it? Who can teach me? I really need to learn the Buddhadharma. Can somebody please tell me more?" He wants to learn, because it's only through learning skillful means (Sanskrit: *upāya*; Chinese: *fangbian*) and then teaching by means of these expedient methods that he is going to be able to get people to wake up.

So, things have changed for the Bodhisattva. This is really a turning point for the Bodhisattva. He realizes that it is by learning the Dharma that he is going to be able to help. The Dharma is the thing that is going to help people wake up. So, he needs to learn it.

It is like a doctor who has learned the basics of biology, chemistry, physics, and the mechanics of the body and is now learning healing techniques. He is learning the applications of medicine. The Bodhisattva is learning internal medicine and external medicine. He is learning the important aspects of spirit and emotion to healing and illness. The more tricks of the trade he can learn, the better he will be at helping people heal and recover from illness. So the Bodhisattva is a Dharma doctor-in-training right now. He's still in "medical school," but at least now he knows what he needs; he's got the basics, he knows what he needs in order to be able to respond to the various illnesses that are going to come his way.

The Four Noble Truths:
Afflictions are Bodhi

Bhikshu Heng Lyu

*A Talk Given by Bhikshu Heng Lyu on the evening before
the Guanyin recitation session at the City of Ten Thousand
Buddhas, March 26, 2016.*

Recently, someone noted that we seldom speak about
the Four Noble Truths here at the City of Ten Thousand Buddhas[3] (CTTB) and asked if that is because it
is only relevant for individual liberation rather than

---

3. The City of Ten Thousand Buddhas is a major Buddhist center and
the headquarters for the Dharma Realm Buddhist Association located
in Ukiah, California.

for the Mahāyāna path. In fact, this teaching also applies to the Mahāyāna path.[4] Here at CTTB, we also practice them in our daily lives. Tonight, I would like to share my humble thoughts about the Four Noble Truths.

The First Noble Truth is suffering. What is suffering? To put it simply, whenever someone or something goes against your wishes, which troubles you or upsets you, you suffer. In other words, suffering is to have problems or difficulties. So, if everything were to follow your wishes and if you could have everything you wanted, for sure you would have no suffering. However, that is impossible. Why?

Because nothing is permanent. For example, you want to stay healthy, but you often get sick and are hospitalized; or you want to have great relationships, but you are a dreadful bore or very annoying; or you want to have eternal youth, but you age year by year; or you want to be rich but you are poor. This will leave you feeling disappointed and depressed. This leads to suffering.

Each person's suffering is different and each individual feels differently toward suffering. Some

---

[4.] Practitioners of the Mahāyāna ("Great Vehicle") follow the path of the Bodhisattva, which leads to Buddhahood, aiming to help others attain awakening too.

suffering is minor and thus endurable, while some suffering is great and difficult to endure. So the degree of our suffering and our understanding of suffering are very subjective. Although we differ in gender, age, race, educational background, upbringing, and economic status, we all experience suffering in our daily lives. This is the First Noble Truth —suffering.

Since suffering is so common in our life, why did the Buddha talk about it? The Buddha talked about suffering in order for us to face suffering with an open mind. This means that we need to face problems and difficulties with courage. Please do not resist or reject suffering with negative emotions. Instead, we need to calm down and face it squarely, so we can really deal with the problems and difficulties. If, in trying to resist or reject suffering, you become angry, complain, curse, become depressed, upset, or pessimistic, it is just like rubbing salt on a wound— it only hurts more.

Not only should we not resist or reject suffering, we should also not try to avoid it. For example, in order to evade problems and suffering, people drink, do drugs, go clubbing, indulge their senses, and even commit suicide. Not only does this not solve your problems, you end up with more problems and suffering than before. This is like in a duel: it is possible to win only if you have the courage to face your enemy.

When the Buddha was a prince and saw suffering from old age, sickness, and death, he didn't get skunk drunk in the palace day after day to evade it. The Buddha also didn't curse and complain, or become angry, gloomy, or depressed nor did he resist or reject suffering. On the contrary, he faced suffering with courage in order to end the problem of birth and death.

However, those who don't understand Buddhism think Buddhism is pessimistic because it teaches about suffering, such as the three kinds of suffering, the eight kinds of suffering, and the myriad kinds of suffering. On the contrary, the Buddha talked about suffering in order to let us know how to deeply understand suffering and then to deal with it with a positive attitude. Therefore, the First Noble Truth is very positive and meaningful.

Since we all experience different degrees of suffering, how do we deal with it and end it? First, we need to understand how suffering comes into being. Suffering doesn't come from nowhere, it has its origins—there are causes and conditions for it. This is the Second Noble Truth—the origin of suffering.

The Second Noble Truth is to analyze and understand the origin of suffering. It is like a sick man who visits a doctor to find out what illness he has and what caused it. What is the cause of suffering? It is our minds, because when people, things, or situations do not accord with our wishes, we become upset, and this is suffering. Since the origin of suffering is our mind, then what kind of mind is it?

We are attached to ideas about how things should be or how people should behave, and if they don't match our ideas, we become upset. For example, you may go to the casino with the intention to make a good deal of money. Such an intention is a cause of suffering. Then, when you lose all your money, that is a condition of suffering. As a result, you get upset and depressed. Therefore, as long as there is a cause of suffering, there will be suffering when the conditions of suffering are present. It is the principle of cause and effect.

Sometimes we are deluded or confused about having to reach some kind of perfection—this, too, is a cause of suffering. This reminds me of a story. A successful businessman travelled a lot, made a lot of money, and owned many large houses. One day on a business trip he was very tired. He saw a man sitting under a big tree at the foot of a hill. He went there to take a rest and asked the man, "What do you do for a living?" The man answered, "I'm a woodcutter." The businessman said, "It's very hard work to cut down trees in a forest. It's better for you to work in a business to make lots of money." The woodcutter asked, "If I have lots of money, what will happen?" The businessman answered, "If you have lots of money, you can own many large houses, and then you can enjoy your life." The woodcutter said, "You see, I work in these beautiful and serene mountains, I already enjoy my life." This story is very simple but its principle is profound.

Some people think they have to be pretty or rich or have some kind of achievement to be liked by others. Then they will be happy. Or, they may think people should respect and admire them. If someone doesn't like them or show respect to them, they feel hurt or insulted. These are all causes of suffering. According to Buddhism, they have a very strong attachment to the idea of a self, and their delusion is heavy. So the Buddha taught us about the Second Noble Truth, reminding us that we must deeply understand the origin of suffering in order to treat it accordingly.

The Third Noble Truth is the cessation of suffering. Using the analogy of a sickness, this means there is a cure! In addition to giving a patient the confidence and hope of recovery, the doctor sets clear goals and a plan for the treatment. All of this provides positive energy to accomplish the goals. This is the meaning of the Third Noble Truth.

The Noble Truth of cessation is founded on the Second Noble Truth, the origin. If we fail to understand the real causes and conditions of suffering, we will have the wrong ideas about the cessation of suffering and go in the wrong direction. In the end, we may end up wasting time and energy, or even worse, we may get what we dislike. You may think, *My cessation of suffering is to win the $150 million jackpot. With so much money, I can enjoy myself in any way I want to, without worries or limitations. I can pursue my dreams and live in comfort. This would be my cessation of suffering.*

However, the Buddha told us that we cannot find long-lasting happiness in external things, because no matter what happens, we will gradually learn to adapt to them. If you win the $150 million jackpot, you may buy a grand new house, a new car, you may quit your boring job, wear fancy clothes, eat expensive food—all the aspects of your material life may improve significantly. But within a few months, the contrast gradually blurs and your pleasure fades.

How does this happen? Your pleasure comes from a huge increase in wealth. After a few months, however, the new comforts have become the new baseline of daily life. Then you take them for granted; you want more money and then you plant another seed of suffering.

Even worse, the money might cause feelings of insecurity because you are afraid of being cheated, blackmailed, or kidnapped. The money may damage your relationships with family and friends. Some lottery winners have been murdered by their relatives for the money. Lottery winners are so often harassed that many have to hire bodyguards or security guards or even move, hide, and end all their relationships. Even though they have money, they are very unhappy. They worry that the money they now depend on, whether it is saved in banks, invested, or hidden somewhere, might decrease or be gone one day. Then what?

In many industrialized countries, wealth has doubled or tripled in the last 50 years. Their G.D.P.s have greatly increased, which has improved their standard of living. People own bigger homes, more cars, TVs, personal computers, and mobile phones. They can afford to dine out more often. Their health has also improved and so has the average life expectancy. However, the level of happiness and quality of life has changed very little, and depression is on the rise.

To end all suffering overnight is very difficult, because we have too many habits and attachments. It is like when someone has many kinds of illnesses. It is hard to cure all of them at once. The healing needs to be done step by step. It is similar with ending suffering. For example, there are four stages of Arhatship. In the course of the Bodhisattva's practice, there is the First Ground, the Second Ground, the Third Ground, and so forth, all the way up to the Tenth Ground, Equal Enlightenment, and Wonderful Enlightenment. These examples represent different degrees of liberation. This is just like any building project. There are many different sub-goals along the way, leading to the final goal of the completion of the project.

After we have set clear final goals and sub-goals, how can we reach these goals? How can we eliminate the causes of suffering and end suffering? We need plans and methods. It is just like a patient who needs treatment to recover. This is the Fourth Noble Truth—the way to end suffering.

What is the plan to end suffering? Besides truly understanding the causes of suffering and the right way to end it, we also need to do it step by step and follow the right sequence of practice. Only in this way can we reach our goal. When we took refuge[5] with Master Hsuan Hua[6], he asked us to bow to the Buddhas ten thousand times to reduce our karmic obstructions, such as arrogance. He also asked us to practice the Six Great Principles to cultivate our virtue and character as the foundation for being a good person.[7] After that, we could choose a Dharma practice of our own, whether it be meditation, recitation of the Buddha's name, mantra recitation, or Sūtra recitation. The idea is that after you perfect yourself as a person, you attain Buddhahood. This is what the Venerable Master Hua designed especially for us and it is the best sequence of practice.

The Fourth Noble Truth is about the way to end suffering. There is a Chinese Buddhist saying, "There is only one road back to the source, but there are many expedient ways to reach it." That is to say, the myriad different ways of practice in Buddhism all

---

[5.] Taking refuge is a formal ceremony where one takes refuge in the "Three Jewels": the Buddha, Dharma, and Saṇghā. The Saṇghā is the community of monks and nuns.

[6.] See "Biographical Sketch of the Venerable Master Hsuan Hua"

[7.] The Six Great Principles are: 1) no contention; 2) no greed; 3) no seeking; 4) no selfishness; 5) no seeking personal advantage; and 6) no lying.

serve to help us end suffering and attain happiness. However, we must first understand our own conditions so that we can choose the appropriate methods, which is like choosing a treatment according to one's illness.

Although the Four Noble Truths consist of suffering, the origin of suffering, the cessation of suffering, and the ways to end suffering, the underlying principles are integrated with each other as a perfect system that can be applied whether you seek your own individual liberation or seek to help infinite living beings. In terms of Dharma teachings, there is no "great" or "small" path—the difference is in your mind. If you have a great heart, you can benefit countless beings no matter what you practice.

Someone may say: "Facing my suffering with courage or an open mind is too painful, too difficult. I can't do it." Another person may say: "My past emotional traumatic experience is too painful for me to face. So how can I apply the Four Noble Truths?" When you raise such a question or have such a thought, you are already applying the First Noble Truth. You are willing to face your suffering instead of running away from it. When you no longer avoid or ignore these issues, you are applying the First Noble Truth.

Next, try to find a comfortable environment, relax your body, and adjust your breath so you can calm down. When you calm down, you can investigate the real causes and conditions of why you don't want to face these traumatic and painful experiences. After deep and careful contemplation, you will find out that the pain is caused by attachments in your mind that you don't want to let go of. If you can apply effort this way and deeply understand the real cause of your suffering, you are applying the Second Noble Truth.

When you understand that the real cause of your suffering is your inability to let go of your attachments, try to think of someone in the world who had a similar experience and eventually rose above it and is now free of that suffering. You will find that there are people who have had similar or worse experiences but faced their misfortunes with courage and now live in peace. You can also try to let go of your attachments and to eliminate the causes of your suffering.

This cannot be done overnight, so you may want to set some more sub-goals that are easier to achieve step by step. This is the application of the Third Noble Truth, the cessation of suffering. When you have goals and direction, you can make short-term, mid-term, and long-term plans. If you achieve your sub-goals in the right sequence using appropriate methods, you will finally achieve your ultimate goal. This is applying the Fourth Noble Truth.

The principles of the Four Noble Truths are the same as the Chan school's[8] teaching that "afflictions are Bodhi."[9] We start by facing our afflictions with an open mind, without avoiding or rejecting them. Then we contemplate and understand the causes and conditions of those afflictions. Next, we establish right goals, vision, and sub-goals for different phases in order to end afflictions. Finally, we practice according to the right sequence to end suffering and return to our inherently pure and bright nature. In this way, aren't afflictions transformed to Bodhi?

---

[8] Chan is an abbreviation of chan-na, a transliteration of the Sanskrit word dhyāna, where the general meaning of dhyāna can be taken as meditation. In the Chan School of Buddhism, the practice of meditation is foremost. Japanese Zen originally derived from Chan lineages with the Japanese character for Chan being pronounced as "Zen."

[9] "Bodhi" is a Sanskrit word that means "awakening."

Mind-Ground Meditation: The Ancient Art of Learning by Subtraction

Martin Verhoeven

An excerpt from Martin Verhoeven's weekly lecture on the Sixth Patriarch Sūtra at the Berkeley Buddhist Monastery, September 19, 2008.

This practice we are doing, sitting meditation, might more properly be called a science of inquiry, and it is very old, having its origins deep in antiquity. We know this to be the case because we have found statues and icons portrayed in this posture dating back to one or two millennia before the Buddha.

The statuary of the *vajrāsana*, the vajrā posture, pre-dates the Buddha by one thousand years or more. Nobody actually knows when it began. It's that old! Nevertheless, we have a pretty good idea of what this practice is all about because it has been handed down generation after generation. I would say that it is basically the most fundamental and profound form of inquiry we as human beings can take up. It's the highest order of thinking we are capable of. And yet, at the same time, it's amazingly simple and straightforward. You needn't make any purchases and it requires no special equipment. You can do it using just what you came into the world with— well, you will also need some clothes, because, though you came into the world without clothes, here we don't do birthday suit meditation! But you did come in with what the ancients call 'your original face', and finding, or recovering your 'original face' is the goal of meditation.

When I first came to the monastery, I asked my teacher, "How do you meditate? What do you do?" Of course, I spoke very broken Chinese and he didn't speak English, but I don't think that is the reason I got the answer I did. He said, simply, "Do that!" and pointed to the statue. But I tried to sit with my legs crossed like the statue's and I couldn't do it. I couldn't even get into a good half lotus, much less a full lotus. So what looked like a pretty simple thing at first—imitating the statue's posture—turned out to be quite difficult. But within the statue itself, in the form in which it's been passed down, are embedded the techniques and the actual methodology of this practice. The texts help to explain it, but only through actual practice can we experience it. I looked at the statue closely, began to study the statue well; and I watched my teacher, and gradually through looking and trying to imitate it I started to connect with it, both within and without. Connect with the statue aesthetically, emotionally, and spiritually, and you will be able to get a feel for the basics of this practice. That is what's so remarkable. Texts may be lost, may be burned in a fire, but the statuary remains, and it functions as a model, a wordless embodiment, for the three essential aspects of meditation practice: śīla, samādhi, prajñā.[10]

I do not mean to suggest that textual study is not important, or can be dispensed with. It cannot. It is a good and wise teacher, but practice itself is also a teacher. You need both teachers; like two wings of a bird. Knowledge of this practice has come down to us in two modes. One is what we might call

---

[10.] Śīla (moral discipline), samādhi (meditation), and prajñā (wisdom) are the three aspects that make up the Buddhist path.

'the inspired embodied tradition,' in which there is a passing on of knowledge from teacher to disciple. The disciple masters the practice, becomes a teacher, and then passes the knowledge on to another, and another, over the course of thousands of years. And that inspired embodied tradition continues into the present, and hopefully will continue into the future. Then there is what is called the received tradition. These are teachings, which have been written down, or preserved by memorization in an oral tradition. An example of this would be the text we are studying now, the *Sixth Patriarch Sūtra*.[11] So, what we are doing here every Friday night is fusing the two traditions. We are taking part in the inspired embodied tradition, which I learned from my teacher, and which he learned from his teacher (and on and on, to the far reaches of antiquity), and, at the same time, we are linking it to the written received tradition, thereby bringing them into their proper relationship: study informs practice; practice lights up study.

I should say now that meditation isn't just a sitting posture; it's a way of life. The texts clearly state that you don't have to sit to be meditating, to awaken.

[11.] An important Chan Buddhist scripture, this text describes the life and teachings of the Tang Dynasty Patriarch, the Great Master Huineng.

They also warn you that you will go astray if you get too attached to your sitting practice, seeing sitting alone as meditation, instead of seeing meditation as a way of life, and your everyday life as meditation. That's why we try to keep both dimensions in mind. The practice of sitting meditation isn't samādhi. It isn't dhyāna. It isn't enlightenment. It's an expedient exercise with which we discipline ourselves and which helps us to get a foothold in a larger process of self-transformation. Sitting is only necessary because we lose our original mind, and don't know how to find it again.

Knowledge of this practice was passed along orally for hundreds of years—let's say from the time of the Buddha—without ever being written down. People went to a teacher, they studied under him or her, they learned directly from a mentor, and they asked him or her questions. And so for about four or five hundred years, there was no written record of the practice. The first written texts on Buddhist meditation only began to appear in the century preceding the Common Era.

Another thing to be careful of is to think that this ancient mental discipline is training the brain, or other modern forms of enhancing memory, retention, neural functioning, or even stress reduction. According to Buddhism, the mind is not the brain, although it includes the brain. So we have to be careful here. One of the Chan questions is: *Where is the mind?* Well, where is it? I don't know!

Those of you who have studied the *Śūraṅgama Sūtra* are aware that this is how the whole exchange between the Buddha and Ānanda begins: Where is your mind, Ānanda? The mind is inside of us. Ok, let's take a look. Not really quite there? Well, then maybe it's outside of us. Not really outside either? Or maybe it's inside of us *and* outside of us? The mind seems to be—in modern parlance—a 'distributed property.' This is an inquiry into something very basic, and yet something, despite all of our advances in knowledge, we really know very little about. It centers on the most fundamental questions, the sort of questions a child might ask: "Who am I? Where did I come from? Where am I going? What is this all about? Was there something before I was born, is there something after I die, and what do we make of the brief interval in between?"

Again, this line of inquiry approaches a science, perhaps an 'inner' science, in that it is concerned not just with the observed, but with the observer, and his or her 'field.' It might be better termed a science of awakening, or as the *Avataṃsaka Sūtra* calls it "the expanding and understanding of the mind and all its states." And both the inspired and received tradition say that there are discoverable answers to those questions. These things are actually knowable, but they are only knowable by you directly, or as the Sixth Patriarch says, 'by yourself, for yourself, in yourself.' This knowledge cannot be given to you by someone else. Nor is it simply accepted as a matter of faith. The answers can be - indeed, *must* be - directly experienced and known immediately. The contemplative exercise of body, breathing, and mental discipline we call meditation helps sharpen the focus of that inquiry. It activates a more refined, sensitive, tool of inquiry within us that reach beyond even words and thought. So in this kind of science you are both the scientist and the subject; the experimenter and the experiment. Your own mind is your laboratory. Conducting this kind of science is very inexpensive, but quite exacting. You don't need to apply for any grants or funding. You have already got everything you need. The exacting part, however, requires a strict and careful application of the right method. Learning alone is sterile; but practice without learning is blind.

What's even more interesting: you needn't take notes or compile data. Nor do you need to publish your findings to validate your findings. In this way, the science of 'seeing the nature,' is the exact opposite of all the other sciences. In all the other scientific disciplines you're accumulating data, running tests, and building up a body of knowledge. But with the science of meditation practice it's the very opposite. Instead of adding and accumulating, you subtract. Subtracting and again subtracting until empty. A text says:

> *Learning consists in adding to one's*
> *stock day by day;*
> *The practice of Tao consists in*
> *subtracting day by day,*
> *Subtracting and yet again subtracting*
> *Till one has reached inactivity.*
> *But by this very inactivity*
> *Everything can be activated.*
> *(Daodejing, chapter 48)*

That's how we activate the higher faculty. That refined sensibility is actually impeded by hyper-activity, so much doing. Over-muchness dulls and lulls it until it drowns. The only way to activate it is through stillness and letting go. We take away, or let drop away, everything that is covering over the penetrating functioning of our true nature. You uncover what's there instead of layering up more. That's why the sitting posture we see in the statuary is a posture indicating stillness, quiet, calm, minimizing of desires and maximizing receptivity.

Most of the time we are projecting our fantasies, fears, and longings onto things. It's kind of like our mind is running a film where images are thrown up on a screen in such a way as to make them seem real. But contemplative practice is the opposite. It entails reception rather than projection. You are shutting down the projective faculties. Your brain, eyes, ears, nose, tongue, and mind fall back into quiet receptivity. And when in your practice you reach a point of absolute, deep stillness, then 'everything manifests by itself.' Hence the saying: "to a still mind the universe surrenders." It is then that you receive the answer to those fundamental questions: "Who am I? Where do I come from? Where am I going?" You don't *think* up these answers; you *see* them. Or as a Chan verse puts it: "unexpectedly the news arrives!"

It all sounds awfully simple, right? But for most of us it will take many years and perhaps many lifetimes of practice to perfect. One, because we have accumulated a great deal of clutter; and two, there is no room for error in perfecting this method. The margin of error here is zero; one cannot be off by even a single thought. Your practice has to be so precise to get the proper result, that if you are just a little bit off, you will miss by a thousand miles in the end. And here's what's really frustrating: if you desire to attain this result, you're off. If you think you've gotten it, you're off. If you fear you won't get it, you're off. And if you even think there's something to get, you're also off. That is why it is said, 'At the place of seeking nothing, there are no worries. Subtracting, and yet again subtracting, you unexpectedly arrive.' So, as you can see, all of this is somewhat counter-intuitive from the point of view of everyday ordinary consciousness, but, nevertheless, it can be done. What's the alternative, really? As a Dharma sister of mine, a Buddhist nun, once said: "there's nothing else to do, might as well cultivate."

Expand the Measure of Your Mind: The Bodhisattvas' Contemplation and Motivation

Reverend Heng Sure

An excerpt from Rev. Heng Sure's weekly lecture on the Avataṃsaka Sūtra at the Berkeley Buddhist Monastery, June 15, 2013.

In the text today, the Bodhisattva contemplates various realms. In doing so, he or she uses another inner kind of vision to look at realms. Now, what are realms? We could spend the entire lecture this evening talking about realms because it is a very big topic. Is it a universe? Is it a galaxy? Last week the Hubble telescope photographed a black zone in space and discovered a hundred million trillion infinite galaxies in this place where they did not think anything existed. Is that a realm?

Let's look at the text: what are the realms that the Bodhisattva contemplates? What are the mindsets that he gets? He "contemplates the realms of living beings": humans, polar bears, caterpillars, birds, kookaburras, wrens, microbes, ancestors—all these realms of living beings, the realms of sentient creatures. He "contemplates the realm of dharmas"—where is that? Everywhere the mind goes there are dharmas.

"Contemplates the realm of worlds." Okay, so now we're getting out there into the cosmos. How do you define a world? Traditionally, this is defined as having a sun and a moon, a polar mountain—Mt. Sumeru—four seas, four continents, and so forth. "The realms of space." Suddenly, we're talking big. The realms of space exist where things are not. It exists in your skin pores, in your blood cells. Open space: the absence of things. So you get it, right?

The Bodhisattva works with these contemplations; these are mindsets that he is looking at in order to prepare his mind to learn the Fourth Ground, the teachings of the Fourth Ground. What is going on? She's expanding her mind. She's getting big so that the information that's coded into this Fourth Ground will go in and take root. When we look at the dessert menu, we're contemplating the realm of dessert. Or we might be contemplating the realm of coffee —whether to get a soy latte with a double espresso shot or to go with the house blend. Those are realms of a different size, wouldn't you say? That is the realm of the tongue. So, the Bodhisattva says, "Yeah, there is a time for the realm of the tongue but I'm expanding my mind to look at living beings, to look at dharmas, worlds, space, to the realm of consciousness. That will make my mind big enough to absorb what I need to learn on the Fourth Ground."

Why? The key is, this Bodhisattva saw suffering; he or she encountered suffering. Along with the suffering, he or she also encountered the deeper connection between me and everybody—not just all people but all beings. Upon seeing that connection with all beings as well as the suffering that beings go through, the Bodhisattva said, "I just can't let that be kind of par-for-the-course. I can't let that be business as usual. I have to do something about it. I can't just let it go. I need to get involved to relieve the suffering." And so with that thought, it became necessary to go out and learn ways to make it hurt less for the beings with whom the Bodhisattva saw that he was connected to. Not helping would just be too cruel. To just look at how other beings undergo suffering and not help in any way, one really has to harden his heart. You have to get very callous in order to see all that suffering go down and just say, "Yeah, that's how it is." Or worse, add to it. So with that in mind, as the key or the framework for understanding this whole thing, suddenly a lot of the Bodhisattva's behavior makes sense.

This is what the Bodhisattva woke up to: that people who he or she cares about deeply are hurting. The Bodhisattva wants to do something about this and therefore started to learn the Buddha's methods for ending suffering, of which there are many. The Buddha himself mastered these methods and is willing to share them with anyone. We just need to put ourselves in a position to be able to learn them. How do you do that? By contemplating the realms of things that expand the measure of your mind. Like what? Like empty space. Like consciousness itself.

The Essential Practice: Mindfulness

Bhikshu Heng Lai

Spoken by Bhikshu Heng Lai at Snow Mountain Monastery during a three-day Amitābha Buddha Recitation retreat, July 2015.

A lot of people, especially Westerners, who want to check out Buddhism really like the idea of meditation because there's no religious commitment. You don't have to bow to anything. You don't have to recite anything. Just sit and meditate and then you get enlightened. It's really straightforward. But when it comes to actually doing Chan, sitting meditation, they find it is not so easy. Master Hsuan Hua used to say, "People who can sit Chan and do it properly to attain the Way are maybe one in a hundred." It is the direct school and therefore it looks simple and straightforward. But because it is deceptively simple; it is actually the most difficult.

I know this because I did the same thing. When I lived at our first monastery, Gold Mountain, I just wanted to sit and wake up. At Gold Mountain Monastery, we would have a recitation session before an intensive Chan retreat.[12] A Chan retreat would last for one to three weeks—sometimes even longer. In those retreats you just sat for twenty-one hours a day; you sat for an hour and walked for twenty minutes. It seemed impossible—how could we do that? It was really hard but it was actually quite doable. I thought, *This is my opportunity. Now I'm really going to wake up!*

So, one or two weeks into the session, I'm grinding my teeth, trying to wake up, and my teacher walks into the Chan Hall, leans over, and asks: "What doing?"

"Shifu[13], I'm trying to wake up," I said.

[12.] A session, or retreat, is a set period of time for intensive practice, generally lasting 7 days. Over the 7-day period, participants will focus on a certain Dharma practice. In this case, participants practiced reciting the name of the Buddha Amitābha.

[13.] Shifu is Chinese for "master" or "teacher" and is how disciples would refer to their teacher.

He chuckled and said, "That's stupid! This is not how you wake up, you just don't understand. Be patient. Don't be greedy for enlightenment. When it is time to sit, then sit. When it is time to walk, then walk. Don't be worried about enlightenment. It will come when conditions are ripe. The more you grasp at it, the less it will come."

I think for Westerners, the best thing is to recite because, although we try to do pure Chan, we're not very good at it. You become good at it if you learn how to recite and bow first, because those are active forms of meditation. The trouble with everybody is that they think that all these cultivation methods are different but actually they are the same. Doing recitation is just Chan. Bowing to the Buddha is just Chan. Chan is bowing to the Buddha, and so is recitation. It is all cultivation. When the Buddha was in the world, there was just one school: the Buddhadharma.

So, now we are doing an Amitābha Session where we recite the Buddha's name every day. We are actually cultivating Chan, according to Shifu. Why? We are building our mindfulness when we recite, so that our mind is right here right now, not yesterday, or tomorrow. We want to just recite. If you do it properly, your whole mind becomes Amitābha. That's it, there's nothing else going on. Yet you are still fully aware; you may hear birds chirping—but it's all just Amitābha. There's a famous saying in Buddhism, that just this here and now is the Pure Land. *This* is the Pure Land. We all look at the Pure Land as some beautiful place up in the clouds where we go when we die. The Pure Land is *right here*. Take a look. It's *right here!*

There's a saying in Buddhism: "Walking, standing, sitting, and lying down, everything is cultivation." You should be mindful. We are building up our mindfulness. Bring your mind to this moment, to this very moment, and your true Buddha nature will manifest. We can do that by reciting the Buddha's name: "Namo Amituofo." That's all you should hear and feel; you shouldn't even think the word "Amitābha." Then you are making some progress.

Outside of this session, we should also treat our daily life—when we walk, when we go to work, when we go to school—as cultivation. Keep building up your mindfulness. It doesn't matter what you are doing, you should treat every day as a Chan Session—or Amitābha Recitation Session, or Guanyin Recitation Session. Every day is *just now*. You build up your awareness, your "now-awareness." The more you build up your "now-awareness," the more awake you become—that's how you open up your true wisdom. It'll just pop out of you, sooner or later, because all of us have it.

When the Buddha became enlightened, he said, "Wow! Every living being has the same nature—it's incredible!" That's the first truth the Buddha spoke: "All living beings have the Buddha nature." But he probably didn't say it that way. He probably said, "Everything has this pure and wonderful nature. We're all just thus." So this is one of the most profound things about the Buddhadharma.

So now we are reciting every day, every hour, every minute—and hopefully we wake up as we do it. Sometimes we wake up a little bit, sometimes we wake up a lot. We don't want to get discouraged. Every day is just a day. You treat it that way: treat it as the only day. There is no yesterday and there is no tomorrow. It is just now.

[QUESTIONS FROM THE AUDIENCE]

Question: This is my first time attending the Buddha recitation session. Usually my Dharma door is Chan or studying the Sūtras. Now, I am having quite a bit of difficulty reciting the Buddha's name. How come it's so difficult to recite the Buddha's name and what should I do now?

Dharma Master Heng Lai: If you are doing something that's truly easy, you'd better take another look at it, maybe you aren't doing something right. Master Hsuan Hua used to tell us, "Cultivation is really hard, and it's really easy at the same time." So, we all feel a little awkward doing different things. *Oh this is my Dharma door, oh that's my Dharma door, oh this is my Dharma door.* We don't even know what our Dharma doors are, we aren't even in that stage yet. You start knowing what your Dharma door is when you start really waking up.

Everybody thinks they understand what their Dharma door is. I used to think that Chan was my Dharma door. Shifu said, "You just follow along, and do everything we all do. Mindfulness is your Dharma door. Be mindful. Whatever trick it takes for you to be mindful, that's your Dharma door. Stop making up all this nonsense." But we would say, "Well, if I do this kind of thing, or I recite that, or I look at this, then I see that, then that formula works for me." "Oh really?" The Master used to laugh at us and give us a big "No!" because we'd get all attached to these ways of doing things.

[14.] Tripiṭika is a Sanskrit word literally meaning "three baskets." These refer to the three parts of the Buddhist canon: Sūtras (discourses), Vinaya (monastic precepts), and Abhidharma (systematic doctrine).

In fact, at our monasteries we practice all five schools (Chan, Pure Land, Esoteric, Vinaya, and Teachings). Shifu was a Tripiṭaka [14] master. He was a master of all five schools of Buddhism. He wasn't just a master of Chan or master of Pure Land. He said, "There's basically no school." And it's the same principle in your cultivation. Don't be so attached to what you're cultivating. I'll do anything. If it's bowing, that's fine. If it's reciting, that's fine. If it's reciting Amitābha, that is also fine. It's all fine because it's helping us build up our mindfulness. That is cultivation, when you build up your mindfulness.

Question: When I recite the Buddha's name, especially when I sit, then I feel my qi and blood circulate and it causes my shoulders and bones to make cracking sounds. The qi also goes up to my head, and then it causes me to lean backward—it's kind of uncomfortable. This happens after sitting for one or two hours, and it has bothered me for one or two years. How can I improve that?

Dharma Master Heng Lai: When we bow or recite, everything we do, we are creating some kind of qi, some kind of energy with our bodies. Master Hua would tell us that when we bow, we are creating qi in our stomach that comes to our heart. When we are sitting Chan, we are also creating qi. There are stories of masters who can actually melt snow because they can create so much energy simply by sitting.

You want to know about a specific situation regarding your own body? I don't have that kind of wisdom to tell you. I can tell you that you should try to accord with conditions; get tuned in to yourself. If you are doing something that's awkward or unusual for you, then maybe change it and do it in a different way. Don't just keep going on. Maybe your body is trying to tell you something. Basically, you should be in accord with your body, like you should be in accord with heaven and earth.

Question: That idea of according with heaven and earth makes perfect sense to me. At the same time, I also know the message, "You have to endure to breakthrough." According to that idea, you have to do what actually feels unnatural, to endure what is difficult, to overcome obstacles. I think there are several instructions in Chan that mention how we need to sit with the pain in our legs, to just have the attitude, "I will not move—you, legs, can fall off!" But then, it seems to me that such approaches don't seem to be in accord with heaven and earth.

One Dharma Master at the City of Ten Thousand Buddhas once told the story of how she complained to the Venerable Master Hsuan Hua about her back pain for almost three years. The Master seemingly dismissed it. But he obviously did not dismiss it; he recommended other things. One day, she realized the pain was gone. But she hadn't done anything in particular. She just happily went along. She couldn't explain it.

I always find myself having trouble around this issue. Someone once told me, "If your cultivation is causing you any discomfort, you're doing it wrong because there should be joy in cultivation. There is a difference between the discomfort caused by the practice and the joy that comes from the practice." Somehow that eventually clicked, yet often times I still find myself struggling with this balance: What does it mean to accord with heaven and earth? What does it mean to break through an obstacle?

Dharma Master Heng Lai: We really accord with heaven and earth once we wake up. *That* is really according with heaven and earth. So, anything before that—we are not really there yet. That is what the breakthrough is all about. *Oh, I'm not according with heaven and earth enough to break through.* How do you know? You don't even know what according with heaven and earth is in the first place. You have to get through your "pale cast of thought." Shakespeare said that. We are controlled by a pale cast of thought. It is like the sky is overcast all the time. We are so used to it, we think that's reality.

The First Stage Arhat, someone at the first real stage of enlightenment, has left all defilement far behind. This means that he has broken through and stopped his false thinking. In fact, all thinking is false thinking. But for us, our dualistic thinking is going on all the time, even about good things. It is like this "pale cast of thought" that Shakespeare spoke of; even he had the wisdom to know that. We are so bound by it. We think it's real, but it's a joke. When you break through that and stop it, then you have the first taste of enlightenment, the first taste of truly according with heaven and earth. You start to feel the anvil, the weight on your shoulder lifts — "It's truly, truly wonderful," so it is said.

Our foxlike minds are always active. Our minds are like lawyers: *If I do that...but if I do this...but, but, but...* It's constantly keeping us in a cycle of thinking, thinking, thinking. We cultivate to get through that. We cultivate to put that to rest, to stop it, to break through it. When you get a first taste of enlightenment, you don't have to ask anybody, you'll just know. You'll know, because we all have this

Buddha nature in us. That's the first thing the Buddha said. We all have great wisdom inside us, we just have to tap into it.

What Counts as Pure Land Practice?

Bhikshuni Heng Chih

*The following excerpts are taken from the September 16, 2015,
"Mechanisms of Practice" class at the City of Ten Thousand
Buddhas. This class is co-taught by Bhikshuni Heng Chih
and Doug Powers. The topic of the evening was Pure Land
practice. In her comments, Dharma Master Chih draws upon
the commentary of a famous Chinese exegete, Master Ouyi
(1599–1655).*

The Foundation of Pure Land Practice: A Profound Confidence

In Pure Land practice, the first thing we have to do is trust ourselves.[15] This basically means that we acknowledge that we have a capacity to be a Buddha and that we have a mind that is neither the physical heart nor cognitive thought. We trust beyond the sixth consciousness and the emotions of the heart—that we have a "true mind." It has no beginning, no end, no boundary. So, we have to believe in ourselves and that's not easy. In the Theravada tradition there is a practice known as mettā —loving-kindness meditation. Have you ever used it? The first thing you have to do is like yourself. That may take a while before you can move on to liking something else.

So, you have to have this trust, this faith in yourself, that even though I'm drowsy and confused, upside-down, deluded, I can, with a simple change of mind, obtain rebirth in the Pure Land because my mind is capable of the perfections of the Pure Land. Basically, Master Ouyi says that we create with our minds this world we're in and all that goes with it. If we can do that, why couldn't we create the Pure Land? That's basically the question.

---

15. A pure land is a land in which Buddhas and other beings live. Here it refers to Amitābha Buddha's Western Pure Land of Ultimate Bliss.

It says in the Pure Land Sūtras as well as in the *Lotus Sūtra* that even if your mind is scattered, even if you're not paying attention, even if you're saying the Buddha's name while you're driving and you're listening to the news at the same time and there are four people talking the car...even if you're scattered like that, you plant a seed with your recitation. There is the beginning of something that can sprout into your being able to go to the Pure Land to become a Buddha. If we focus on it, at least through certain times of the day, then how could we not? Of course we should be able to get there.

Pure Land Practices

Let me tell a story about one of the monks who was here for twenty-eight years and went back to lay life. He had a lot of self-doubt. It was his self-doubt that eventually led him to disrobe. But he was a good monk. You see, the first step in metta practice, trusting yourself, is very important.

One time he was about to go to Canada. Before he went, he asked if he could do a repentance. In the old days, when my teacher, Master Hsuan Hua, was around, you could do what was called "Baizhong" [literal Chinese: "tell the whole assembly'']: a public repentance. You know how we are all the hero of our dreams and tend to put all the ugly things way down inside and just forget about them. But what happens when you're around someone like the teacher we had, Master Hsuan Hua, is that they surface. Maybe he pulls them out, or maybe he creates a situation where we pull them out ourselves. And then you're stuck with them: there they are. And so we would come to the point where we would want to repent of them. It is taught that you can repent for past mistakes and then they're done for, they go away. So this is what he, Heng Tso, wanted to do. A lot of us did it. I myself did it several times: it is a magical time. You would have to get the Master's permission, although he did not necessarily know everything you would say.

So the moment came for Heng Tso to do his public repentance. He expressed his usual kind of self-doubt again. You know, "I'm no good, good for nothing; I can't really..." But he had the courage to say out loud all the things he'd done wrong. Whenever such a repentance started, those of us who sat around and listened, would know with the very first sentence that this guy or girl was going to tell it like it was, and that it wasn't going to be easy. It wasn't going to be easy for them to say and it wasn't going to be easy for us to hear—and THAT was very magical. When I was the protagonist, when

I was the one doing it... *wow!* I can't even describe what that was like to get rid of that burden. And the other thing is that everybody knew: they knew your worst thing, which is what spouses or good friends are supposed to be able to do, they're supposed to be able to know the worst thing about you and still support you. But in a public repentance you say them to the entire assembly and if you are honest and true, everyone will support you.

So, Heng Tso did that, he told all of us his worst things. And then he said, his conclusion was, "So I'm not good for anything else; I am going to practice Pure Land." Shifu, our teacher, rarely praised anybody. I only have one praise in my book for my whole life with Shifu. *[Laughter from audience and a chuckle from Dharma Master Chih.]*

That night that monk got his praise. That night Shifu said from his high seat for all of us to hear, "Shan zai, shan zai, shan nan zi. Very good! Very good! Good man." We were all just *shocked. [Laughter]* We didn't hear that very much. Shifu gave a little commentary. He said, "For someone of your age, a young American, to be to be able to pick this up, to trust Amitābha and trust yourself and do this practice: incredible!"

Heng Tso then asked a very good question, he said, "What are the Pure Land practices?" Obviously, holding the name of Amitābha is a central Pure Land practice. Great Master Ouyi taught not to do anything else, to just concentrate on reciting the name. But Heng Tso asked, "How about the Great Compassion Repentance? Does that count?" "Yes," Shifu said, "because Guanyin is on the right of Amitābha in the Pure Land." He further asked, ''How about the Great Compassion Mantra or even the Śūraṅgama Mantra?'' Actually, if you go into the Śūraṅgama Mantra, you'll find lines that refer to Amitābha in the West over and over again. The Universal Door Chapter that we recite and bow to during Guan Yin sessions also counts as a Pure Land practice. The Master confirmed, one by one, that these can be counted as Pure Land practices.

To be honest with you, I am not somebody who holds Amitābha's name all the time. My practice has been to hold mantras and meditate. When I meditate, I use the topic ''Who is mindful of the Buddha?'' Where does that topic come from? For people who hold the name in their daily practice, you are mindful of the Buddha. Somebody who is really good at this holds the name *all the time*, whatever they're doing—sweeping the walkways, eating, sleeping, cooking; they are always saying Amitābha's name. But when you go into the Chan Hall, you don't. You don't sit there and say "Namo

Amitābha, Namo Amitābha, Namo Amitābha''—
you don't. You ask yourself, "Who says 'Namo Amitābha'?" When you're practicing in that way, you
look for the self, the false self. That is my Amitābha
practice. It is the reverse of reciting his name; instead, it consists of looking for *who*. To be true, that
is the way I've done it. But I have also recited how-
many Universal Door Chapters, bowed how many
Great Compassion Repentances, recited the Śūraṅgama Mantra and Great Compassion Mantra who
knows how many times. If we go by how Master
Hua answered Heng Tso that day—and that is inde-
lible in my mind and probably for anybody else who
heard it—those all count as Pure Land practices.

Meditating on "Who am I?"

Bhikshu Heng Lai

Spoken by Bhikshu Heng Lai at the Buddha Root Farm
Summer Retreat on August 12, 2012.

In the Chan school, one of the methods is holding a meditation topic (Chinese: hua tou). These are often questions. The most popular one simply asks "Who?"

Question: How do you investigate the meditation topic "Who am I?" Do you contemplate it intellectually?

Dharma Master Heng Lai: When you say the word "me," or "I," or "who am I?" you start thinking about that question, and how ridiculous it sounds. *Who just asked that question? Who am I? Who said that? Who?*

That is what is meant by "dwelling on your hua tou." It means, "Who just said that? Who's asking the questions?" That is what you're supposed to be dwelling on. It's a short circuit. These two wires are short circuiting against each other. *Who am I? Who just asked that? Who am I? Who said I?* That's what you think about. You are not supposed to recite the question like a mantra. Instead, it becomes a burning thing in the back of your head. If you have real success in Chan, then this becomes a burning question. It is called the "great doubt."

I had this happen to me spontaneously at sea once. I didn't know anything about Buddhism, but it just happened. It was a great doubt. It was more like a great big cloud. It came over me, and it was like a weight. That's the way I can describe it. It was as if this huge weight was on my shoulders. *What is this all about? Why am I here? Who's asking these questions? Who am I?* I didn't know I was working on a hua tou, but I was. But then it became more and more intense and it just stopped. Everybody has a different experience, but in my case, all my thoughts stopped for a second. Probably more like a microsecond, but it felt like a long time. That moment, I saw all things as they really are, without any thought in between.

We suffer from thought. The texts speak of the ground of the joy of leaving defilement. This defilement is our thinking—even pure thinking. Any kind of thinking—good, bad, and ugly—is false thinking. And no matter how sophisticated your thinking is, it is nothing compared to when your thinking stops, to seeing the pureness of things as they really are. And for me, there were no fire-crackers or light shows, I didn't see Guan Yin[16] descend from the heavens or anything like that. I was on watch, and I was looking at all these stars, and they were just "thus, thus." Everything was just the way it was. And it was a profound relief. I started crying. It was really beautiful. It was as if somebody took an anvil off my shoulders. I just went, *Ahhhh*. It was really joyful. And I wanted to go grab the people I was on watch with and shake them and say, "Hey look! Look!"

Then I started for the first time feeling the real frustration the Buddhas and Bodhisattvas feel. They can't make people see that. They have to trick

---

[16] Guan (Shi) Yin is one of four Bodhisattvas with the greatest importance in Chinese Mahāyāna Buddhism. Known as Avalokiteśvara in Sanskrit, Guan Yin is the Bodhisattva of Compassion.

people into seeing it. You have to use expedient devices. People have to attain it themselves.

In my case, because I had no foundation at all, my mind didn't stay that way very long. I think within a week or so all aspects of that experience were pretty much blocked back down again. This caused me to go into a deep depression because here was this enormous joy and relief and then all of a sudden, it's back again, all this false thinking, my mind covering it all up. I couldn't even stand up straight, I was so depressed. I was in Majorca, an island off Spain. Our ship pulled in there and when I came ashore, there were all these leather goods on display. They sell all these leather coats—leather, leather, leather everywhere. So, all I could see were the skins of living beings. It was all I could see. And the horrible smell of their skin! I thought, *Oh God, I'm in the hells. What is this? This is awful.* And then I found a Catholic church. Catholicism is thousands of years old in Spain. It was an old, old church. I went inside to take refuge from all this leather everywhere and from all these people. When I got inside that church, it was very peaceful. There were all these cultivators in there. Who were they? Old ladies. They were reciting with their beads. And because they were cultivating, they were purifying. They didn't know it, but they were cultivating a Dharma door. It was very peaceful in there. I just stayed there, and it was really nice. Then I decided, I've got to find somebody to help me because I don't know what to do about this. I knew I couldn't talk to a priest. They would not be able to answer these questions. That's when I started getting interested in finding a guru or something. I needed somebody to explain what had happened to me.

When you have an experience like that, your priorities shift. You are no longer interested in anything in the world. All this, everything in the world, is trivial. I realized that everything here, which everybody thinks is so important—it's just total bananas! I knew that I was never going to be interested in anything, but that I really needed to find somebody to help me with this great question, this big thing that happened to me. That was my situation.

Going Home: The Only Journey is Returning

Martin Verhoeven

An excerpt from Martin Verhoeven's weekly lecture on the Sixth Patriarch Sūtra at the Berkeley Buddhist Monastery, September 19, 2014.

Tonight, we will finish up the third part of the introduction to sitting meditation by talking about what one tries to do internally as an introspective exercise in getting a handle on the mind. Last class, we went through the physical points. First, the seven points of the foundation of good sitting posture. Then, we went through the breathing component. At the end we stressed that the breathing works naturally itself when the whole body is very natural and relaxed. It is an effortless kind of breathing similar to the breathing that you do when you are resting or even asleep. Good meditation breathing takes care of itself.

As for the mind, we need to apply some effort, but not too much. Just as with the breathing, there is a natural 'tending toward' of the mind; it naturally tends to purity and stillness. This naturalness is what the classic texts point to as the true nature of the mind, or the innate tendency of consciousness. That is, although sometimes Chan (Sanskrit: *dhyāna*; Japanese: *Zen*) is translated as 'stilling the thoughts' or 'calming the mind', these translations can be somewhat misleading. A meditator is not so much actively 'calming and stilling' the mind as letting it be itself or return to itself: naturally calm and still. It may seem like there's not much difference between "doing it" and "letting it be," but there is, and it is right on this point that we can easily go wrong in our practice.

The Sixth Patriarch's *Platform Sūtra* is very helpful because the text tells us that the mind fundamentally is calm, still, quiet, alert, yet at the same time nowhere attached. We have an inherent disposition— that Huineng[17] describes simply as the *nature* or *self-nature*—for clarity and stillness. You don't really calm or still the mind so much as not allow it to ruffle and stray, or worse, to run amok. When the texts say, "walking, standing, sitting, lying down, do not separate from *this*," it means do not leave or depart from the true mind's natural stillness and purity. The effort applied then is in letting go, releasing our grip and grasp, rather than striving to get hold or acquire. My teacher once started a week-long meditation session with this verse:

> *Living beings grasping everywhere*
> *Cover over the wondrous.*
> *Let go! Release your hold:*
> *The wondrous revealed!*

The language of meditation can be a little misleading. This is not just a problem of translation or semantics. If, in the actual practice of doing this, you think that you have to stop the mind, quiet the mind, either gently or forcibly; or that you are trying to stop thoughts, and 'cut off' all mental activity, you will get frustrated and easily feel defeated. You have

---

[17.] Great Master Huineng (638-713 c.e.) also known as the Sixth Chan Patriarch of China had his life and teachings recorded in *The Sixth Patriarch's Dharma Jewel Platform Sūtra*.

to think outside the box a little bit, in the sense that —if the texts are right, if the Patriarchs are correct here—the natural state of my mind is in itself pure and still, and its unobstructed functioning is to see things as they really are.

In fact, Venerable Xu Yun (English: Empty Cloud) and the other great teachers all say that just 'seeing the nature' is the whole of it; meditation came about only as an expedient for those of us who could not just see-through things and 'put it down,' or let go of the false. In seeing things as they really are, you recognize that there is not one thing that you can get, attach to, or cling to. Any sense of 'getting' or possessing is an illusion; or, as the *Heart Sūtra* says, in this deep state of liberated wisdom, "There is no knowing or obtaining."

One master called reaching this state of understanding "attaining nothing to attain." This is not, however, to suggest we live in a state of denial and renunciation; that would just be another kind of attaching. Rather, it is being centered and clear, attuned to just how things actually are. But this should not be mistaken either for indifference and apathy. The best expression for this dynamic equilibrium is from the *Platform Sūtra* where Hui-neng tells his disciples to be "everywhere engaged, but nowhere attached."

So you just have to let the mind happily rest in this state of awareness, and not let it run off on a shopping spree, chasing bubbles and illusions nor let it slip into a nihilistic dull emptiness. The ancient masters were quite clear on this point: The meditation exercise is secondary, not primary. It is only necessary as a counteractive technique to get back to the ground that is 'fundamental' or 'basic' to our natural state of being. It may not now seem natural, but that is because through neglect compounded by habit, we have become so disturbed and so stirred up with this business of grasping and seeking that it has forgotten its true 'home,' lost its way and even the confidence that it has the ability to return, to recover it. So meditation is not seeking enlightenment, or even advancing; rather, it is more like coming home. Maybe that is what Laozi means by "In the Tao, the only motion is returning."

Sometimes at this stage in the journey you need faith. If we use the word "faith" in its active, not passive, sense, it is a dynamic conviction, or transformative insight, or a moment of clarity within in which you realize, Ah, I have really strayed far from my deep human roots, my true self, sometimes poetically, "the wind and light of my original home". This faith is a kind of spontaneous sureness that comes unsought for and cannot be denied; sometimes they call it a sort of 'inspired clarity': a moment of self-knowledge in which you really know you have that innate ability. You don't so much *believe*, as you directly *see* that you have that nature, whole and complete. Even if seen for a moment, it changes everything.

This is the meaning of "the sea of duḥkha is vast and wide; but just a turn of the head is the other shore." It's a foundation, a kind of tenuous foothold on solid earth that allows you trust your own footsteps in the Way. This confidence may not be deeply anchored yet, or fully formed, but you know it is there in the 'deep heart's core,' as the poet said. The next step is using that "faith." Faith is not something you 'have' but something you 'do.' 'Doing' faith is an engagement, a determined resolve, to reclaim that space, to restore that ground. This faith is very active; not simply saying, "I believe," but insisting, "I can; I will." Faith is not a static or outward hoping for deliverance. Rather, it is an inner stirring born of a profound change of heart based on a moment or moments of clear seeing, followed by a resolve saying, *I am going to, I believe I can, and I will go back to that state. There's nothing else worth doing!*

From clear seeing then comes this resolve to return. It can produce an indescribable joy, a pure pleasure, because you know you are in the heart and throb of what it means to be a person. You have trued your bearings and you know it. You are honoring and reclaiming the deepest part of your nature. This joy starts to arise naturally. It is not a happiness that comes and goes: *Oh, today was a good sit and I feel good, and yesterday was a bad sit and I felt bad.* No, it just comes from doing the work, from knowing that you are engaged in the real work of becoming fully human, in something timeless that is deep and genuine. This resolve acts like a catalyst, releasing a kind of joy that doesn't come from any place or anyone outside, but from an inner alignment to what is most deeply and intrinsically authentic, pure, artless.

I want to stress this point again, that when we're calming our mind and stilling our thoughts, we really aren't actually exerting that much effort or striving to attain some transcendental high. The purpose, and the aim the texts point us to time and time again, is that we need only 'to light up the mind and directly see our nature.' The light is already whole and complete within us for this task, if we just don't let it dribble away and scatter its bright focus. This is why the *Platform Sūtra* says, "Let the mind be unattached, clinging to nothing"; let it be itself, as it naturally is, 'thus'; do not seek outside. Do not wander or stray from your own natural stillness and purity. Walking, standing, sitting, or lying down, do not separate from 'this.' There is a sense of firmness this brings. But faith in a way also makes you feel vulnerable, because it's all about letting go, releasing our grip and ungrasping.

So, meditation is not something you *do* really, but something you do *not do*. Some texts call this *wu wei*, literally "not doing." This is the meaning of the line, "With not a single thought conjured up, the true nature of reality manifests." Or, as the *Śūraṅgama Sūtra* says, "When the mad mind stops, that very stopping is awakening." It's a different approach than 'seeking' enlightenment.

So, in the technique of sitting meditation, you borrow fire to fight fire, or as they say, 'use poison to counter poison.' The untamed mind can stir up a lot of waves in the originally calm, lucid sea of consciousness; over time these chaotic waves seem normal. We habituate and can easily forget that our mind was ever any different from its present tumult. This habit energy is like the flapping wings of a hummingbird; all we see is the blur of motion, we cannot see the wings themselves. Once stirred up, the true mind is hard to recognize. It is constantly moving without direction, wildly grabbing without ever getting hold of anything. It is sometimes compared to the wind coming up with storms or compared to a turbulent river flowing—eddies, and cycles, and currents, and waves just going all over the place. You would think that water could never be calm when you look at a river like that.

This process of calming the mad mind is, as the famous commentator, Tang dynasty monk, Chengguan, Master Qingliang (738-839) said, like dealing with a fire. When you observe the fire, you see this constant activity of burning, but you can't tell where one flame begins and the next one ends off. It is just ceaselessly burning in this fashion. It doesn't seem to have any control and nothing is determinate. There is no causation and no end point, until there are ashes, and then another fire starts. This scholar-monk also compared the mind and its wanderings to a turbulent stream or the capricious blowing of the wind. He gets even more specific— he says that "one breeze doesn't know the next. One wave doesn't know the other wave and it is being pushed along, yet it doesn't know it is being pushed along, and it is simply following. It is not really following the one in front. No one can tell where this will go". This is consciousness untamed. This is consciousness gone wild. And yet, this very same consciousness tamed is bodhi, awakening. Awakening is described not as something we get, but as someone we become; it is not transcendence, but transformation. And it is found right within the here and now. This is what the texts tell us.

The goal in the meditation practice, at least at the beginning, is simply to observe the workings of the mind, to closely watch over the ground of consciousness as described in this passage. This is just getting to know yourself. As my teacher used to say, "Simply, with a calm and even mind, observe the rise and fall of conditioned phenomena."

Watch as every impulse, emotion, longing, fear, etc., arises, crests, then falls away. They come and go on their own; they cannot be held or had. By not repressing or giving in to them, but just 'watching,' one begins to see all that frenetic activity for what it is: dreams, illusions, bubbles, shadows. So the first stages of meditation my teacher would describe as somewhat akin to a being a dummy, but what he meant by 'dummy' was not stupidity but a kind of 'cultivated foolishness' that comes from not madly seeking after what all the world seems to value: name and fame, power and glory.

If we can become 'dumb' in this way, if even for a moment in meditation, that momentary stopping brings the mad mind into bold relief. For a moment in the meditative exercise, you can actually see your mind at work, as the quiet sitting allows its noisiness to be heard almost at full blast. It can seem that your mind has become more active, even more wild, than when you were not meditating. It has not. It is just that you just never paused to take a close look, to isolate and observe the field of consciousness.

Sitting meditation, at least in the beginning, only provides a background or a platform from which to see one's own mind. It sort of freezes the frame and allows for a closer look by way of contrast. But this look, however unsettling, is extremely important and valuable. Otherwise, you are just always being pulled along like a bull with a ring in its nose. (Not everyone is of course familiar with this metaphor. I apologize. I spent my summers on a Wisconsin farm and was very much afraid of the bulls; they were so big and powerful and not docile. But my uncle showed me how they were subdued: A bull could be led by a rope tied through a ring piercing its nose. Even I could do it once I held the rope securely).

When we actually start contemplative practice, the first sensations we may have can be overwhelmingly chaotic. It's not that the meditation is causing this, but only that the meditation is exposing what is already there: all this frenzy, frenetic activity going on inside. You might say, *Well I must be practicing wrong, or this monastery is no good, or the teachers and their dharma methods are really deficient.*

As a matter of fact, this inner tumult can be seen as an efficacious response, because we are seeing our mind in the wild, uncultivated, unrestrained state we have let it slide into. People experience this in varying degrees, and the degree to which we experience it is a measure of how unruly our minds have become. The more it has gone to seed, the wilder and more unmanageable it seems when you sit. The task of quieting the mind seems almost impossibly daunting, beyond reach, like a puny David facing off against the giant Goliath. You might fear: *I can't ever subdue this!* Or to use another Western allusion: you might feel hopeless like Sisyphus doomed to roll this immense boulder up the hill, only to have the rock roll back hitting him, again and again. It isn't hopeless, but it can be hard. I felt this way when I first began practicing. I asked my teacher if there was some secret method or special technique, he could impart to make it fast and easy. He smiled and said: "There is no shortcut; there is only patience and hard work. Don't look outside!"

His words seemed harsh, but true. Patience is only possible if you have a reliable and true method. I knew I had that. It was the "don't look outside" that really hit home, though. And here, it seems to me is the key: that very ground and no other is the only ground we have to work with. Cultivation can seem hard or easy depending how far we have strayed, or how badly we have neglected the ground of our nature, but there is never a point of no-return. As Mencius put it "rightly tended, no creature but thrives; neglected, no creature but pines a way." It was the mind, the nature, he was talking about.

However, even if we have strip-mined it, clearcut, drained it nearly dry with overuse and abuse, it can be restored. So, difficulty in the beginning of meditation is to be expected. It is not our original state, nor our fate or destiny; but it is a true reflection of what we have become. And our current condition, whether we like it or not, is the only ground of awakening. My teacher would constantly remind us of this bittersweet fact. He might say, "there may be a road in heaven, but you cannot get there without walking the road right under your feet," or "the long, 10,000-mile journey begins with a single step on the ground right below your shoes."

Even if you don't experience difficulty, you have to be equally patient and suspicious of early ease. For example, you might enjoy moments where you actually can sense this natural calm and clarity, even though it still ebbs and flows. Or, you may feel light and cool, floating on clouds. But do not think this is 'enlightenment' or something special. Big mistake. On the other hand, you may not have any far-out states happen, and imagine that others do and that you are falling behind, or not making progress. But don't get nervous. Meditation is not some kind of competitive game, or a contest to show that some people's minds are better or more deserving than others. That is not the case; the mind is universally the same in all beings. All beings have the potential for this awakening. Some come back slowly, some quickly; but in the end and all along there is no fundamental difference. The mind of a Buddha and an ordinary person are not different, just differently realized. Huineng, the Sixth Patriarch, hammered on this point:

> *Buddhahood is realized within the essential-nature; do not seek for it outside yourself.*
> *Confused, the self-nature is a living being;*
> *enlightened, the self-nature is a Buddha.*

There is a famous poem by Tao Yuanming (365-427) based on this realization that begins with the metaphor of going home. He must be sixty years old at this stage and he's lived a pretty interesting and wild life. Suddenly he realizes that he is completely out of control, there's little time left, and that he is just being pulled along by his habits and impulses. He writes:

> *I am going home! My fields and*
>   *gardens are choked with weeds.*
> *Why should I not return?*
> *My mind has been my body's slave;*
>   *how sad and lamentable!*
> *I realize that the past is gone, but I can*
>   *certainly rectify what is to come.*
> *I have not actually strayed too*
>   *far from the path.*
> *I have awakened to today's rights and*
>   *yesterday's wrongs.*

In the first line of the poem, he says: *I'm going home*. In other words, he is going back to this fundamental 'ground.'

The second line says: *My fields and gardens are choked with weeds*. This describes how through the neglect over time he has allowed his mind-ground to be overrun and neglected. The Sanskrit term for this is *kleśa*. But, he says, *Why should I not return?* That is the third line, the turning. This points to his determination and faith: *I see it, I'm going to go back, oh my gosh, I've really let this thing go to seed*. Note: he doesn't despair, but just rolls up his sleeves and goes to work. He says his mind has been enslaved by the body. He could have equally said, 'my body's been my mind's slave.' The mind can completely be imprisoned by sensual indulgences, but so can the body become a pawn of the confused thinking and pretensions of the mind. Regardless, the poet does not wallow in guilt of the past, nor postpone to some fantasy future, but just attends to the here and now.

My teacher used to point us in this way: "When one attends to the here and now, the false returns to the true." His last line is key: he hasn't strayed too far; in fact, if the texts are correct, we can never leave the 'path' completely, because the Way is not outside, but is our very essence, our fundamental nature.

The idea is that you clearly recognize, okay, that's my ground. You don't judge it, don't get insane, or fret, thinking *I'm just so sinful and negligent, and I've led such a wild life, oh woe is me. . .*and then sink into despair, and maybe even a little bit of self-mortification. Guilt-tripping, wallowing in shame and self-effacement are not Dharma principles. If you go that way, you can paralyze yourself. Remorse should be a catalyst for change, not a death sentence. Otherwise, what began as a healthy admission of error, can easily turn into crippling confinement. So, we don't go there, as too much regret becomes another affliction; choking the garden with more weeds. Yet, not enough regret can easily turn into a different kind of paralysis: arrogance and indifference. What we need to do is, like a doctor, look objectively, almost clinically at ourselves; do the diagnostics, and take the medicine.

Tao Yuanming is very much in the spirit of Buddhism. But other thinkers express a similar sentiment. Look at Ralph Waldo Emerson, the 19th century American transcendental philosopher. In his essay on self-reliance, he talked about how all we have to work with is 'this' [tapping his arm for emphasis], ourself, this is the ground that we have to work with, there is no other ground. He wrote:

> *There is a time in every man's education when he arrives at the conviction that envy is ignorance; imitation is suicide; that he must take himself for better or worse as his portion; that though the wide universe is full of good, no kernel of nourishing corn can come to him but through his toil bestowed on that plot of ground which is given to him to till. The power that resides in him is new in nature, and none but*

he can know what that is which he can do, nor
does he know until he has tried.

Counter-intuitive as it may seem, in this 'walking the Way' we don't get anything by grabbing, seeking outside, taking shortcuts, or cheating; nor is it a matter of luck, or chance, or magic. Emerson, like the Buddha, says that the soil that's given you to till, this natural ground, is all that you have to work with, and all you need. Nobody knows what they can do, or will do, until they try. All of this, though written centuries after the Buddha, is in keeping with his teaching and the Sixth Patriarch's exhortations to cultivate your own person, realize bodhi directly by, for, and through yourself, and not look for it apart from the ground right under your own feet.

In the first stage of this meditation, when you sit, you are gathering in your body and relaxing your breathing: gathering in and centering. Then you take up one of the various mental exercises, called 'meditation topics' or 'one-pointedness'—well-established techniques for steadying, holding, settling, watching, observing the mind. They all differ slightly, but have the same purpose, to free up the mind from habituation and clinging. The American poet Robert Frost had a wonderful way of describing freedom.

Someone once asked him, "What is freedom?" Without a moment's hesitation, the poet replied, "To me freedom means riding easy in the harness." Using precepts and a meditation topic is "riding easy in light harness."

Liberation in the Way is not unrestrained abandon, but bringing the mind under light harness; holding precepts and countering distraction, keeping focus without letting the mind stray or wander. This 'stopping' itself is not the goal, however much it might be appealing, even seductively stressless. It is just the first phase in opening awareness, insight. These focusing techniques gather back the light so that you can then see more clearly and penetratingly. That's the meaning of "return the light; illumine within." You will see exactly what is there. Then you will know what you have to do.

After a while, you start to recognize recurring patterns of thoughts, feelings, emotional reactions, habits, attitudes, and so forth. You can experience all kinds of memories, recollections, flashbacks, involving not just images, but corresponding emotions, even smells, tastes, tactile and emotional feelings. Things will stir up that you think you have forgotten, because quite a bit is stored in this deep layer of consciousness; called the *ālaya-vijñāna* in Sanskrit, meaning 'storehouse'. The mind is multi-dimensional and interfunctioning; at some level it acts as agent of change, and a repository for all your thoughts and feelings, for all the karma that we've enacted with body, speech, and thought over such a long time. Past, present, and future all converge here. This is a huge gigabyte, terabyte, mega-terabyte, MEGA-mega-terabyte, whatever storage thing that doesn't have any capacity limit! So, it is all there. And you *could* go on filling this thing without ever maxing out its capacity.

Well, in order to let it return to its home, all of that stuff has to play itself out, or be 'crossed over,' as the text says. Or to use another metaphor, these residues of karma, both wholesome and unwholesome, are like seeds lying dormant in the mind, and when the necessary causes and conditions come together, they manifest (flower) into an active, explicit form. This is one meaning of "everything is made from the mind alone." If left untended, these patterns continue to play themselves out. This can be fascinating, but also a bit tiring. But these patterns also can be changed. Meditation provides a narrow window of vision, and momentary opportunity to not just react or be pulled along blindly by one's karma, but to skillfully adjust and alter its tendency and intensity. Either way, none of this is permanent or fixed; it is just like a river rolling on and on. But unless we understand the dynamics of it all, we just bob and sink in the whirlpool. One text, the *Visuddhimagga*, describes it as:

> *No doer of the deeds is found,*
> *No one who ever reaps their fruits:*
> *Empty phenomena roll on:*
> *This view alone is right and true.*

> *And while the deeds and their results*
> *Roll on, based on conditions all,*
> *There is no beginning can be seen,*
> *Just as it is with seed and tree.*

Interestingly, none of these states want to stay; they have no nature of their own, no will. They are empty, but we keep feeding them, giving them artificial life. If not fed, they evaporate just like morning dew by afternoon. Unless we keep bolstering them, they possess no life of their own. This is one of the meanings of "all dharmas are not-self."

So, between the two extremes of reacting and giving in to them, or repressing and fighting with them, meditation offers a third possibility: simply observe their rise and fall. Keep to an unmoving stillness, and they come and go by themselves. Each will then exhaust itself. This is like how a wave comes in from the ocean and hits the shore. Where does it go? It rolls across the land and stirs up the dirt, right? No, it goes *phht*, it's gone. But then the next wave comes in. And it too goes out. Eventually, if you don't keep stirring up the water, those waves will play themselves out. And the water will return to its natural stillness again. So it is not like you quell the waves or still the whitecaps. You simply refrain from stirring it up, stop splashing around, so to speak, and eventually the waves cease and the water settles into an even calm. Because the waves are empty to begin with; and the tendency of water is to stillness.

Patience is very important here. If the theory instead were to say that you have got to squash those waves, you got to press them flat or put a lid on them, then you are going to take a whole different approach to your meditation. But if the basic Dharma theory is correct, you can be patient, realizing that eventually, to use another metaphor: the fire will extinguish itself when the fuel is gone. If you don't rekindle it, if you don't add more fuel and blow on the fire, eventually even the embers will subside. This is one of the images used to convey the state of nirvana: a cool, natural stillness and tranquil equanimity. The fire's out.

This is really important to understand, otherwise we can wind up going really wrong in our meditation. Impatience: we can sink into frustration and throw in the towel when our mind refuses to be 'empty and still.' Or worse, aggression: because nothing seems to work, no mantra or counting breaths or koan or hua tou, will make it stop, we lock into a kind of forceful, uptight repressive meditation. We think, *Damn, I'm going to get enlightened today. Grrr!* If you have that kind of repressive energy, you won't get it. Because that is like adding airplane fuel to the fire. The harder you push it down, the stronger it rises up. That kind of energy is explosive, like *wow!* —but also destructive. If you build a fire, add the force of wind to it, add strong will to it, it can become destructive.

Instead, what you have to do is not be fazed; patience is required, the patience to let it be without repressing and without reacting. Don't try to push it down, and don't try to engage and follow it; whatever arises, just let it come, let it flicker, and let it pass. And when everything has been emptied in this way, not because you *emptied* it, but because you see that all conditioned dharmas are by their very nature ever and always and all along empty, and that there is basically 'not one thing' to get, then you are home; the return is complete. Although 'coming home' is called 'true emptiness,' it is not really empty. Rather, it means our essential nature has been, and is already ever whole and complete, with nothing lacking and nothing needed. This is perhaps the meaning of the expression, "True emptiness is just wondrous existence."

Assault on the Self: How to Deal with the Arising of Karma

Douglas Powers

An excerpt from Doug Powers' "Buddhism for the Modern Mind" class at the Berkeley Buddhist Monastery, May 23, 2016.

The basic problem in dealing with emotions is karmic. You not only have to not be attached to what is arising in the present, but you also have to, slowly but surely, as the past is arising into the present, get rid of it thought by thought and feeling by feeling. After all, you have this huge history of feelings and emotions and those are all constantly arising. So one of the major aspects of cultivation or samādhi is that you patiently wait for them all to pass without reacting to them, because every time you react, emotions arise and are reinforced. So, basically, in terms of difficult emotions, you have to not only not react in the present, you also have to patiently wait out all of the past.

Likes or dislikes, pleasure or displeasure, is all karma from the past that is coming into the present. So, the only way you're eventually going to be able to move past the karma that is already in motion is patience. Even if you were to sit in meditation, in super samādhi meditation, as soon as you come out of that samādhi meditation, the past still has not been done away with. And as soon as your mind opens to it, once again the past will emerge and you have to be patient with every aspect of the past as it arises in the present. That's why the pāramitā of patience is so important. You have to be really patient with your mind, really patient with your body, and really patient with not moving as thought and emotions arise.

Emotions that are occurring are all experiences of the past welling up in the present. Every current moment is basically a neutral experience that is taken over by association with the past. There's not a single emotion that is not generated this way. So, emotions don't happen to you. You have to attend to them when they arise. And if you don't attend to them, they have nothing they can attach to. If the mind isn't moved toward the emotion, the emotion has nothing to attach to and disappears like a bubble. But if the mind goes toward the emotion the moment it arises, if the mind picks it up and tends to it, the emotion then begins to take over the consciousness. You are not controlled by emotion. Emotions are experiences of the past coming into the present and the only way emotions have power is by attending to them when they arise in the present.

So, if you could really develop samādhi in the present, if you could really develop an awareness, then you could actually not be moved by any emotion that arises and could actually choose every emotion. There's absolutely no reason why you wouldn't choose every emotion that you want to attend to.

If you're not choosing your emotions, you're an idiot because you're allowing the emotions to take over the space of your consciousness. We're all idiots. We have to be really careful because if we don't understand that, then we actually think that these emotions—likes or dislikes—are actually something that is happening to us. We might even think we are those emotions. That would be really sad. But they are neither happening to us nor what we are, because the consciousness has to attend to them for them to actually exist. The more distance, the more space you can create, the more stillness you can create in your consciousness, the more power you have over the freedom of your mind.

You're meditating or reciting to create a stillness in your consciousness you can use to not be moved by habituation. That's what you're doing. The point of practice is to create a freedom of mind that doesn't have to be moved by habituation from the past so quickly. It can actually see the process of choice-making that is occurring. Every split second the mind is actually making a choice to attend to something with its attention, and by the choice of its attention creates the experience that you're having in any given moment. Your experience is the attention of the mind on something, it's not actually happening to you.

Question from the audience: Sometimes I get angry and the anger fills me up before I even get a chance to respond. I'm not even cognizant of the fact I'm angry until I'm in the midst of the anger. Once in a while I'm able to see that emotion welling up inside me and I think, "Oh, this is arising in me." I can't say I make the decision not to be angry, but I don't engage in it and it actually dissipates by itself. I think this sort of speaks to what you were saying just now about choosing whether or not to engage the mind in certain emotions. In the first situation where anger consumes me so quickly, I don't even see it happening, what is the momentum that carries it forward so that it consumes my space?

Doug: The momentum is habituation. It's the power of habituation. In fact, going to something like anger, there are many choices the mind has made before it gets to anger. Remember, there has to be some sort of irritation and the irritation is somebody messing with ME, somebody does something or makes some comment or acts in a certain way, and the irritation is the movement of the mind of being disrespected, disregarded, etc., and we could go through a hundred reasons why that happens.

If we look at the mind when it first moves toward the emotion, behind that we'll find attachment to the view of self. There's no anger that doesn't come from an attachment to the view of self. Guaranteed. I guarantee you that at the heart of every single anger you've ever had was an irritation based on the view of self that was messed with in some kind of way or another. Your theory of self, your attachment to a self or some idea of someone you thought you were was being messed with. So, if you could watch the self constantly, your theory of self, your sense of self, of who you think you are—if you could watch where that ends, then you could actually see the moment of irritation and even choose to get irritated or not.

So first of all, you could choose to not even have a view of self. Now, granted, that's pretty deep, to watch from the place where the self-first emerges. That's pretty deep, but it's possible. If you were really meditating, you could actually watch for your "self" being moved. If you're not at that level at least you could watch where the irritation is arising. And if you can catch the irritation where it is arising, then, if you can be patient with not engaging in the irritation through recitation or samādhi or whatever method you're using, that irritation loses its momentum.

Once your irritation has arisen, then it escalates. You could actually watch it escalate in yourself, you can watch it move from feelings to thoughts to body, and even if you catch the anger while it is still in the process of your own self before you said anything else or have done anything with your body to someone else, you still have control over the karma. But as soon as your body has acted on the anger, now you've lost control over the karma.

There's a huge difference between the moment that the anger arises and has even reached a fairly high level within yourself, and the moment you take action on its basis, because as soon as you've taken action, now it's going to be up to someone else. You've lost control over the karma. Now that karma's gone out into the universe, and it's coming back. And as anybody knows in here, a moment of anger could actually fundamentally change your life very easily. It doesn't even have to get to the anger where we are shouting out or something; it can get to a lack of feeling in a relationship, for instance. A moment of anger could have a huge impact and what's said from that moment of anger could have a huge impact on the amount of trust, care, and everything else involved in the dynamic of the relationship. A certain amount of anger could actually change the level of trust, the fundamental level of trust in a dynamic situation between people; it could fundamentally change the karmic conditions.

We have to make distinctions all the way from the first movement of the mind. From that first moment all the way to an action, when we finally get out our guns and start to shoot them all the way down the road. So the degree to which you have enough stillness that you could observe from is the degree to which, earlier in the process, you can catch it. The reason it reaches anger right away is because those places that are habituated—for example, with your dad, whatever he said that irritated you from the time you were seven years old, or when he takes that action or says that thing—the habituation is so great that the immediate response is anger, because it is habituated over time. All these immediate angers are habituated. They are histories of habituation. They move so fast, you can't see them. The boss thing, the wife thing, the parents' thing, the kids thing—you know, they are habituations of some context that have already been built in. The speed of that is the momentum that you were talking about.

Precepts: The Meditator's Map

Reverend Heng Sure

An excerpt from Rev. Heng Sure's weekly online lecture on the Sixth Patriarch Sūtra, March 4, 2016.

Precepts are a lot like a map. The Buddhist precepts, or standards of ethical conduct, are mostly the same for Jews, Catholics, Protestants, and Muslims. That is, they are universally understood to be the basis for good conduct in the world. For example, let us examine the Ten Commandments. Four out of the Ten Commandments are analogous to the Buddha's five precepts for laypeople, with the exception of the fifth precept, refraining from intoxicants, which is not specified in the Ten Commandments.

The guidelines for ethical behavior function like a map. If you just start walking aimlessly, you are going to waste a lot of time. You won't know where you've been. You won't know where you're going. You could wind up back where you started and get nothing except exercise. However, if you have a map and you know the direction you're traveling, you can actually go from San Jose to Cupertino, Cupertino to Palo Alto, Palo Alto to South San Francisco, South San Francisco to the Golden Gate Bridge to Marin County, and wind up at the City of Ten Thousand Buddhas, because you are heading north.

The precepts give you guidelines for behavior. For example, I didn't kill last year, I am not killing this year, and I don't expect to kill next year. Day after day, I do not take life with my hands, with my teeth, or in my thoughts. There are many people who never considered themselves killers, but bit by bit, by cooking animal flesh, slapping mosquitoes, spraying insects with poison, etc., etc., they thoughtlessly commit many acts of killing.

Consider this: "What I am is what I've done. What I do, I will become."

All the three periods of time (past, present, and future) are included in this phrase. "What I am is what I've done." If you want to know my past lives, look at me right now. Do you want to know my future lives? Look at me right now. The things that I have done have made me who I am right now; what I do now is creating my future. "What I am is what I've done. What I do, I will become." There's a lot of wisdom there. Past, present, and future are all included in this idea of cause and effect. This is called "cause and effect through the three periods of time."

Instead of thoughtlessly following instinct in daily life, you could ask yourself, "Where is this going to take me?" Then we could even apply the Six Guidelines of the City of Ten Thousand Buddhas right here: No fighting, no greed, no seeking, no selfishness, no pursuing personal advantage, no lying.

These Six Guidelines are a checklist. Before you jump into a behavior, you can ask yourself, "Was this motivated by fill-in-the-blank?" Look at the impulse. If you are a meditator and have just a little bit of space, because you've been watching your thoughts rising and falling again and again, you can ask yourself, "Is this a fighting thought?" If not, it would probably be good to do; go for it! Ask yourself, "Is this a greedy thought?" If not, it is probably good to do, so go ahead. "Is this a thought full of seeking or am I content?" If it's not seeking, there is probably no harm. "Is this a selfish thought? Is this a thought benefiting me alone?" If you are not thinking just about yourself, it should be okay. "Is this a dishonest thought? Is the motive here to cheat?" If it is not, go right ahead.

The Six Guidelines, which Master Hsuan Hua praised so highly, are a checklist. A meditator who has some awareness, who has some skill in watching thoughts rise, checks with that list of the Six Guidelines as the thoughts arise. If you are not operating based on fighting, greed, seeking, selfishness, personal advantages, and dishonesty, you go for it, you grab that behavior and put strength behind it. It is not the case that Buddhists never do anything, that we are inert and non-committal, and always afraid of this or afraid of that. I know Buddhists who are effective in the world, powerful people, who apply themselves with all of their strength of heart, arm, and brain to good causes. They know their own motives, and know that their motives and actions are not leading to affliction.

Most people face everyday afflictions, not just occasional evils. If we act from a motivation of greed, fighting, seeking, selfishness, personal advantages, and dishonesty, even on subtle levels, then down the road, frustration will result. It won't be satisfying; it won't hit the spot. When the seed is off, the initial motive for behavior is compromised. It wasn't *zheng* [Chinese for], solid, strong, and true. It was *xie* [Chinese for], crooked, off-center. The further we go when we start with a motivation from a place of affliction, the more crooked it gets. The further away from the destination we travel. The positive thing about the Six Guidelines is that when we put them straight, when we are sure that something starts out right, the further we go, the stronger, deeper, the more solid it becomes. So if we apply the Six Guidelines to any situation that is unclear, they will help us make sense of that situation. Body and mind will be solid and cared for well.

Keeping Cool During the Christmas Holidays: Engaging with Family as Spiritual Practice

Douglas Powers

An excerpt from Doug Powers' "Buddhism for the Modern Mind" class at the Berkeley Buddhist Monastery, December 14, 2015. This was the last class before the winter holiday. Speaking directly to the situation of the students in the class, Doug addressed the challenges that come up for many people while visiting family during the holiday season.

Christmas is coming up soon. So you will all have the chance to really work on your filial respect, to really cultivate. From the point of view of cultivation, looking at how well you were parented is actually almost a secondary issue to the amount that it has affected the fundamental ground of your habituation. Seeing through that in an honest way is really difficult.

To me, that is the reason Master Hua pushed filial respect so much. He did so as a Chan teacher. It was not a Chinese cultural thing. It came from the recognition that from the standpoint of Chan cultivation, you need to be connected to your parental construct as much as possible, because then you can actually see that material to work on. The further you remove yourself from that material, the more unconscious it will be, and the more difficult it will be to work through, no matter how positive or how negative it was. Is everyone with me? The basis for filial piety is not a moral obligation, it is a personal-growth obligation to being honest with yourself about those aspects that are embedded in your personality, about your reactions that go back to childhood.

For almost everybody, the holidays become an opportunity to come face to face with those habits and constructs. It's got two sides to it. First, it challenges you: all these old habitual patterns come up when you are around family. Then, on top of the problem of coming back into contact with all these family members, there is the problem of expectations. That is, the second big problem is that people create massive amounts of expectations for each other, that *sometimes* don't get totally fulfilled.

For example, you might be all "charged" with the expectation that someone is going to have a certain kind of reaction to you, or give you some kind of joyful, really exciting, positive time. But when we get into the situation it's not always exactly what our expectations are. So these expectations that don't necessarily get fulfilled can create a lot of suffering. If you're going to make the holidays work in terms of our relationships with people, then the only way to do so is to bring forth your pāramitās: your patience, your careful listening, your gratitude, your generosity.

You know what the number one Buddhist practice that you want to bring forth in December and January is? It's generosity. Generosity will get you a long way in changing your own energy and spirit, and providing the positive energy for your own heart to be involved in a positive way. It also ignites other people's hearts rather than their judgmentalism. If you would just have generosity, the amount that that will do—both in terms of your own exchange on the mind-ground and also dealing with the circumstances around you—will be incredible. You will also need patience.

And if you actually want to communicate, the key is to listen. Careful listening. We've talked about this a lot. A fundamental issue from the standpoint of cultivation, in terms of relationships, is suspending your own interpretations and listening really carefully to what the other is saying and then relating to them through their own context, rather than through your expectations. You can tell how well you are cultivating by how well you are able to suspend your own interpretations, judgments, and emotional reactions. Listen to somebody else and actually accord with the passing conditions of the other person rather than your own reactions. You can always tell how well you are doing in cultivation by how irritated you get.

The really, really great Bodhisattva is the Bodhisattva of irritation [*laughter from the audience*], because whenever you're irritated it shows that the Big Self has been again mistreated—YOU! Other people being mistreated can get you a little excited, but YOU being mistreated, that's a different issue. And that usually creates this irritation. If you can catch the irritation and be patient before it gets momentum, this is really all that practice is. We can do all the practice we want but it really comes down to these things. How patient can you be in the conditions that would have caused you irritation in the past? The second big Bodhisattva is judgmentalism, because as soon as you are judgmental you already know, Oh! The Big Self has arisen once again. The illusory self the Buddha was talking about arises not as an intellectual abstraction, but arises in your mind-ground every time judgmentalism or irritation arise. These are signals that tell you there is still a lot of attachment and so forth. They give you information about where you are at.

You can go all day doing just fine until somebody does a particular thing and then you get irritated. If you look into that irritation, you will see that the ground of that irritation is the illusory self. Every time. A hundred percent of the time. Not ninety-eight percent but a hundred percent of the time. YOU were mistreated. YOU were not recognized. YOU were irritated. Something happened in which you were engaged—something negative—and then on the basis of that, irritation arises, anger arises, actions arise, and then down the whole pathway to like... Well, you know what kind of mess you can get yourself into. So, it seems like this is a good month to practice generosity in the place of judgmentalism, patience in the place of irritation.

For the next few weeks people will be in very different contexts than they are the rest of the year. These gatherings offer a really good chance to see how you're doing. What is really interesting is when you're in a situation where you go back to somebody's house—your parent's house, your relative's house, your brother's or sister's house—that you haven't been at for a while. Because then you actually do see what changes you've made or not made in the passage of time by the way you're reacting to things, to the day-to-day activities of the people you don't see very often.

You don't see your day-to-day changes very much in normal circumstances. But when you go into a situation that you're very familiar with but that you haven't been in for quite a while, that's one of the few places in the process of your year where you can actually see if you've made any headway on being a little bit more patient, a little bit more gentle, a little bit more still, listening a little bit better. At those moments you can really see if there has been progress in your practice.

Does that help? Anybody have any questions?

A woman from the audience: I have a question. I encountered an issue back home. My brother fights with his wife and it's due to...

Doug interrupts: And they're the only couple that does that out there?
[*Laughter from the audience.*]

She continues: I can see why it is, um, because I can observe it. But you always say to only take on whatever I'm ready to take on. And I know the cause of their fighting, but he cannot realize it. Do you have any suggestions?

Doug: I think with your relatives, more than with anyone else, you need to be very careful about trying to engage change. Whereas in friendship there is a chosen relationship—in other words, you have chosen at one level or another to engage in taking care of each other —with family, you're not choosing. It is a given and that makes it much more fraught.

Remember what I said earlier: everything that happened in the past, the diaper-changing they did for you when you were little and so on, is always there in all these family relationships. You may look at yourself as you think you currently are, but remember, they're seeing you through the entirety of their experience with you: from your childhood through all your different personalities and adolescence; they saw all that stuff. You're coming to them as an adult, but remember, they've seen you through the entire process. A brother or sister has been through all those battles, through all that history, so when you come to those relationships with some idea that you're going to change something, it is really fraught.

I don't think that people are very successful in trying to bring insight to their parents or brothers and sisters unless they have a lot of time, and unless the siblings or parents have asked, or given you permission. I don't think that you'll find it very useful to try to engage in the issues in your family, to think that you're going to bring change in your family unless you're asked to. And even if you're asked to, I'd be very careful about it.

I think that with parents, there's only one approach you can take, and that is: engage them within their own value construct, in their existence, in their way of doing things. Engage them inside of that as much as possible, and give positive feedback to what you see as the positive elements of their values, using their own language, their own terms. And in no way think you're going to provide a new insight from outside their construct into their construct, because I think you'll meet with resistance.

Whereas, if you engage them in their own construct, in what you see as a positive value, and you give support for that, especially if you could find something that they have really done well or if they changed something that you noticed and you give them super-positive reinforcement for that, and they get the glow of your recognition, I think you can go a long way with that. But I think trying to engage them as a daughter knowing something they don't know, or trying to help them to understand something, is a dead end: I think you're going to find that very frustrating. [*Laughter from the audience.*]

For many, many good reasons you'll find that frustrating. I highly suggest that you don't try to do that; that's what I mean by not taking on something for which you haven't set up the conditions.

Now, if you're living with your parents, you have time, and you're engaged in their lives, that's a different issue. You might then have an opportunity to engage them. But if you're just visiting, then it is just about the warmth of the relationship. For them, you are their daughter. You are very symbolic for them, very symbolic of things in their ongoing life and future life. You have to understand that as people get older they get more and more sentimental about you, their child. Then the grandkids, oh my... then the symbolic value is all over the place. That's why they're pushing so hard for the grandkids. I don't know if I'm answering your question.

She replies: Yes, thanks.

Doug: Does anybody else want to add something before we move into other stuff?

Another audience member: I just want to say briefly that I spent the weekend with my brother whom I haven't seen in a while. And everything you say is completely true.
[Audience laughs while Doug says "Okay."]

Doug: Yes, well siblings have a lot of history. You have a lot of history with your brother, and with all your other family members. But it's the same principle in all relationships.

As a practitioner, the way you practice with the illusory self is not as a theory but in the actual listening and according to the conditions of the other. Every time you closely listen and accord with the other's conditions without a position outside of that, and agree as much as possible with everything that he or she is doing, unless it really crosses some incredible line that you're not willing to cross, most things will go pretty well. In supporting their construct, it also gives you a chance to practice less self while giving them positive reinforcement within their own construct.

Someone else from the audience: So, you said that, for example, when engaging your parents, you should provide positive reinforcement or things that you feel are positive?

Doug: Yeah.

Audience member continues: What about when they do something that you consider to be negative?

Doug: I usually would say nothing. I really think you want to support the positive things and not do anything about the negative. I do not think you want to negatively reinforce the negative. I do not suggest you positively enforce something that you see is negative. But you don't have to say anything.

For example, they might be getting drunk every Friday night. You're sitting there and they're getting drunk. It is not your place to get involved in their personal stuff at that level. But you don't necessarily have to say, "Oh, this is really great that you're drunk." You do not want to give your support to things that you don't support, but you don't have to be negative about them.

Someone else asks: What if you observe someone saying something whereby he is undermining someone else, not you. What can you do?

Doug: You have to be SUPER careful to engage in correcting anything. Hopefully, as a cultivator, when you look at a situation like what you are talking

about, when you see somebody mistreating somebody else, you're taking a few deep breaths and looking really carefully at what you could constructively
do. You don't react emotionally at all and have no
personal judgment or interpretation that's playing
into it, because any personal thing is going to create
more problems than there were before. Any emotion
will probably make the situation worse.

So, as a cultivator facing something like that,
you take a bunch of deep breaths, you observe really closely whether there's something you could actually do constructively, and you're strategic. You're
neither emotional nor do you make it into something personal. Neither your own personal reaction
nor emotion enters, because if it does, you'll increase
the fire from what it was before. It's not going to
necessarily resolve anything.

Now, even if all those things are in place, I
would still say that it is very important to be strategic. You ask yourself: *Can I really engage in this?
How would I do it? How would I do it the best? Could
I take one person aside, not get into the thing between
them at all but get support for the person who's getting
the criticism, either right at the moment or little bit
afterwards? Could I resolve it later in another context?*

But, the key thing as a cultivator is that you use
the same principles over and over again: you don't

engage emotion, you don't engage view, you're just engaged tactically. So, you'd have to look at the situation and see whether you can make a positive difference or whether you're just going to blow something up into another level of conflict.

From the audience: Wow, that is not easy!

Doug: Well, if it were easy, we wouldn't be all fighting each other, right?

The Low Down on Bowing

Reverend Heng Sure

An interview with Rev. Heng Sure conducted by Loc Hyunh.
Originally published in Dharma Mirror, Fall 2005.

Since the third century CE to this day, bowing to the Buddha
is the most common practice for Asian Buddhists. However,
among Westerners, bowing practice, as compared with medita-
tion, is not as well-known.

Last summer, I had an opportunity to speak with Rever-
end Heng Sure, the director of the Berkeley Buddhist Monas-
tery, and asked for more information about Buddhist bowing
and repentance. In the late 1970s, Reverend Sure and a fellow
monk did a three-year bowing pilgrimage for world peace along
the coast of California. Their journey began in Pasadena
and ended three years and 800 miles later at the City of Ten

Thousand Buddhas in Ukiah. And most astonishingly,
their knees had already endured over a million bows....

Loc: Would you describe the purpose and benefits of a bowing practice?

Rev. Sure: Bowing, like other Dharma practices, can be considered a technology. It's actually a method for changing one's consciousness. And because it's a Dharma practice, it works by using the body. It is true that Buddhism emphasizes the mind; however, we often use the body to get to the mind.

A renowned Chinese monk from the Tang dynasty, Master Chengguan, explained that bowing reduces pride, teaches us respect, and increases our goodness. Bowing awakens these qualities within, affecting our conscious state and view of ourselves and place in the world. The technology of bowing, from his ancient description, is precise. He considers bowing as a medicine, an antidote for pride. It also teaches respect because when we bow, we are physically down on the ground and this potentially allows a feeling of reverence to emerge in our hearts. Bowing increases goodness because the "self" shrinks. Things that we do with a reduced sense of self—and we're not talking about low self-esteem, but things we do without the big "ME" in the middle—tend to turn out better.

Bowing is the first of the ten practices recommended by Samantabhadra (Universal Worthy) Bodhisattva, one of the four revered bodhisattvas of Mahāyāna Buddhism. Bowing is a foundational practice, along with generosity and ethics, for preparing someone for a spiritual life.

Loc: Buddhism does emphasize reducing arrogance and pride.

Rev. Sure: Bodhisattvas in the Buddhist Sūtras, no matter how high their position, all still bow to the Buddha. That is, everyone up to the stage of Buddhahood still bows. In America, our cowboy culture gave us the "self-made man," the independent individual, who says, "I don't kowtow to no man." That can become, "We don't listen to no country, we don't need no allies, etc."

The developed world has machines that tromp over the earth and other species. We consume and cut down forest, dig up minerals, and somehow feel it's our given right to kill other creatures and eat their bodies. Those unwise attitudes result from an inability to humble the self and live in harmony as part of a larger community of living creatures on the planet. The flipside of pride and arrogance is isolationism and loneliness; we do not feel at home wherever we go. Hence, as a culture, we can definitely use a method that can ease this sense of loneliness.

Loc: Did bowing for three years on the California highway deepen the connection you have with people along the way?

Rev. Sure: The longer I bowed the more connected I felt. With each bow I gradually saw a certain sameness in people's faces; I felt a kinship with the people I met. I stopped feeling separateness and, with that change in my perception, people's responses to me changed too. I saw that underneath the exterior, there is a profound family relationship shared among people, animals, and all living things.

The first pictures of the planet earth taken from space showed a tiny blue marble in an inky black universe that stretches on forever and forever. Looking at those photos we realized that all creatures are like people in a lifeboat together. We share the water, temperature, and climate. We are a family; some in furs, some with horns; some have wings and some have scales. Our skins are different colors and our mouths speak different languages, but we all share the same elemental makeup of earth, air, fire, and water.

Bowing shows you this organically. With each bow, the self slowly disappears. In the future, I hope to keep bowing to "finish the job." Most of us don't think to bow; it's so slow and boring. People often asked, "What are you gonna get out of that?" Kids get bowing right away. It feels good to bow. Adults often take longer to try it out. For adults, if they can get through the first couple bows, often it feels so good to lower the head; it feels as nourishing to the spirit as water on dry plants—it's very healing.

Loc: I have some friends who just got back from a three-week bowing repentance session at the City of Ten Thousand Buddhas. Can you tell us more about this event?

Rev. Sure: Every spring the City of Ten Thousand Buddhas (CTTB) convenes a three-week bowing session, called the Ten Thousand Buddhas Jeweled Repentance. During this event at CTTB, we bow to the names of 11,111 Buddhas. This Dharma practice is based on the Sūtra *The Buddha Speaks the Sūtra of the Buddhas' Names.*

Bowing together in ritual movement with six hundred people, moving to music for eight hours a day, creates a powerful catharsis. Those who have tried this ceremony know that the first day, you can think you're going to die from so much bowing. The ego really resists being lowered so much. On the second day, you don't doubt it, you know you're dead. On the third day, metaphorically speaking, we really die, the ego has given up and gotten with the program. But after the fourth day, we're reborn, so to speak, and bowing becomes effortless from that time on.

Loc: What kind of effects does bowing in repentance have on the body and mind?

Rev. Sure: Bowing a repentance liturgy is designed to bring to consciousness the negative things that we may have committed in the past. Bowing changes the blood flow to the upper body, particularly to the brain, and it seems to dislodge memories or thoughts that may be buried in the mind or in our kinetic memory. Seated meditation doesn't function the same way because sitting is stationary and our blood circulation slows down.

When we bow, we place the head on the same level with the heart. The flowing blood and changing energy stimulates and washes clean the effects in the psyche of deeds we have done with our body, mouth, and mind. While bowing, memories and thoughts of all kinds come to mind, thoughts that may be terrifying and embarrassing. They arise because the act of bowing relaxes the muscles from the shoulders, the small of your back, and the chest; it exercises the stomach muscles and the diaphragm, which also hold muscle memory. Attitudes and buried or repressed thoughts we can no longer "stomach" naturally return to awareness during bowing.

Loc: What prevents your bowing from just becoming purely mechanical?

Rev. Sure: If we are bowing in repentance, we can use a verse from the *Avataṃsaka Sūtra*:

> *For all past bad karma,*
> *Created by beginningless, greed, anger,*
> *   and delusion,*
> *And created by my body, mouth, and mind,*
> *I now repent and reform entirely.*

Each bow helps us confront and let go of memories. The power of this technology comes from a combination of physical, psychological, and spiritual elements. Essentially, the repentance allows us to say, "Yes, I made a mistake and, yes, I won't do it again, I'm sorry." When negative memories arise and are repented of, they lose their power to block our consciousness and impede our moving on to healthy spiritual growth. Venerable Master Hua described the process as "Big disasters become smaller disasters; small ones disappear."

Bowing without an attitude of sincere repentance will not be as effective; bowing with sincerity helps clean up our stuff inside. The Buddhas and Bodhisattvas taught the Dharma to help people like us to leave suffering behind and, ultimately, to gain freedom from birth and death. The method of repentance helps us change and transform our minds.

Loc: How does the doctrine of "emptiness" apply to repentance?

Rev. Sure: The self works like a hinge pin on the structure of karma. If the view of self is gone, then there is no place for offenses to land or to stick. By emptying out the self with each bow, and here I'm using empty out as a verb, "to empty out," gradually we can actually change the outlook of the self, the big "me" in the center. If the thing that does good and bad deeds is not entirely in charge, if the agent that does deeds is gone, and ultimately doesn't exist, then how much the less do the offenses themselves exist? And if we can then repent of the mistakes we have made, then slowly we turn the balance sheet around. Offenses are reduced, merit and virtue increases.

If we are determined to change and become like the Buddha, and want to transform afflictions and change the direction of our life, then repentance and bowing are good methods to do so. Bowing is slow and dull but it works to clean the mind's closets.

Loc: How can people new to Buddhism or people who cannot attend long retreats apply the Dharma of repentance?

Rev. Sure: When I was a student, I was uninterested in reflecting on what I was doing. As a student, I wanted experience—the more action the better. And when things happened to me, I was unlikely to say to myself, "Oh, that bang on the head was the result of something I did." My attitude was, "Ouch! Darn! Bad luck!" Then I'd take an aspirin or drink the pain into oblivion.

I didn't have a clue that I might benefit by reflecting and changing my behavior. It's not easy to take that first step: to listen to myself and think things over.

But when we start to practice, and if we get some instruction in the principle of cause and effect, we can understand that things that happen to us are repercussions set in motion by our own behavior. What happens to us is the harvest of seeds we planted.

The next step is to learn how to move from passive understanding to conscious control. Upon reflection we make sense of behavior by comparing with a standard. The Dharma teaches about the Ten Evil and Ten Good Deeds, a set of ethical standards. The Ten Evil Deeds guide us to refrain from creating unwholesome karma with the body, speech, and mind:

Body: Three mistakes with the body include killing, stealing, and sexual misconduct. Instead of killing, the Ten Good Deeds exhort us to be kind to all creatures. Instead of stealing, we are guided to be generous and to appreciate what we have. Instead of sexual misconduct, we are encouraged to be true to our commitments in our relationship and to cherish our body and energy. The world's major religious traditions are unanimous in teaching that irresponsible sexual behavior leads to emotional confusion and heartbreak. Further, careless emotional entanglements make it difficult to find stillness in the mind.

Speech: There are four evil deeds done with the mouth, so the Dharma guides us to refrain from lying, gossiping or schism-making, harsh, and frivolous speech.

Mind: As for the mind, there are three evils: greed, hatred, and delusion. Delusions refer to false views—seeing things the way they aren't, and believing things that are not based in reality.

The Ten Good Deeds are a Dharma standard by which we can judge our behavior. If we observe and reflect our conduct in harmony with their guidance, our actions will yield positive results and we will harvest a life that we want to live.

Loc: And when we make a mistake?

Rev. Sure: When we make a mistake, the first step is, again, to see cause and effect at work, to understand that we are creating the world we're moving into. Secondly, reflect and catch ourselves in our habitual, unmindful, and unskillful actions; and third, from understanding and seeing our actions, we become empowered to take action and change.

We then resolve to change our negative behavior to the positive and in this way to benefit the world. At this point, we will be on the spiritual path and will be using our life unselfishly. Our journey will lead us to meet with wholesome friends and good things will arise out of that community.

Stay Inspired: Advice for Sustained Practice in Daily Life

Bhikshuni Heng Chih

An interview with Bhikshuni Heng Chih by young Buddhist practitioners at the City of Ten Thousand Buddhas, conducted May 2, 2016.

Question: For me and for many our age, the main issue is stress and being too busy. How do I make sure I reserve enough time in my daily life for rest, relaxation, and spirituality? It almost seems as if I barely have any time for that or no time at all, even though I'm surely not always using my time in the most meaningful or productive ways.

Dharma Master Heng Chih: I would say that in such a situation, you should not push yourself too hard in terms of practice. So, I would say pick some practices you like and don't try to do more of them than can easily be done in a day to start with. And then enjoy it. Stay positive about it.

But, I'm going to walk you through the Seven Limbs of Enlightenment, which is the perfect thing for this first question. So, what happens is, there are seven parts to it. The first one is mindfulness. You use that to determine what the following steps will be. After that, the following three are (2) choosing a method, (3) being vigorous, and (4) experiencing joy. You can use these when you're feeling depressed because these are uplifting. Pick something you like, do it, and then, because you like it, the outcome will be you get happier—so you're not so depressed.

The other three of the Seven Limbs of Enlightenment are: (5) letting go, (6) concentration, and (7) renouncing. Letting go is getting rid of the stress, nervous energy, or the tendency to be hyperactive. Concentrating is getting quiet. Renouncing means giving away the positive benefits, sharing them with living beings. It also means to relinquish the habits that create stress in the first place.

So, what you do is you use mindfulness in your day and you figure out whether today my mood swing is depressed or hyper. Then, based on that, you apply these—it's a little psychological method that you can do all by yourself.

So, the answer to this question is that you have to find ways to let the stress go. It takes two to tango. If you don't want to be stressed, you don't have to be. Then to quiet down, either meditate or sit quietly or do something you like that concentrates you, and then give away the positive energy once you get it, while also relinquishing the habits that cause you to become stressed and hyperacitve. This practice is the one I use mostly. I assess myself in a day or sometimes in the middle of a meeting. The whole room may change—we're in the middle of a class, the whole room will change and then I try to figure out, "Okay what should I be doing here? Am I getting stressed by this or am I getting depressed by this?" And then I apply the appropriate set from the Seven Limbs. It works.

Question: We're still relatively young and hopefully have many more years of practice ahead. In what ways can we build the ground for our future cultivation?

Dharma Master Heng Chih: I see the answer to that as being precepts.[18] Because if you really want to hang around and really want to do practices, precepts are the most basic thing.

It is very valuable to commit to them, because when you commit to them, you get help. Every precept has five spirits and those spirits are in the paths of rebirths. The various spirits that protect precepts, protect meditation, and protect people who recite mantras because they made vows to do so. So, you're getting help when you take the precepts. When somebody transmits them to you, you're getting help even above your own capacity, because you're getting help from those entities that have vowed to be good spirits and protect these things. Same goes for bodhisattva precepts; every precept has five spirits. The precepts, you could say, provide you with a protective shield that will create the conditions for you to continue your practice.

And the other thing to say is, if you want to sustain yourself, you have to be happy. It's not to say that you won't have ups and downs, like I've just described, that you won't have doubts about things

---

[18.] The basic Buddhist moral guidelines are the five precepts: no killing, no stealing, no sexual misconduct, no lying, and no intoxicants.

and so forth, but if you really want to sustain yourself you've got to find a way to like what you're doing.

So, I would suggest that the other answer to this question would be to pick practices that you're interested in exploring and try them out, and if you don't like it after you've tried it awhile, pick another one until you find some that really resonate with you. If we don't like what we're doing, it's hard to stay with it.

Question: Over the course of a long and sustained spiritual practice, practice all too easily becomes routine. The joy, inspiration, or even the sense of urgency fade. What do you use to keep yourself going and to stay inspired? In your experience, what is the most important factor in maintaining constancy and a fresh attitude in long-term cultivation?

Dharma Master Heng Chih: I've never really had a lot of trouble with this personally. For me, it's never been a problem because I find meditation absolutely fascinating, and I find the study of Sūtras fascinating and I love to translate—there just isn't enough time in a day.

So based on my experience, I guess the answer would be again to keep a positive attitude. Probably the most important thing is to be happy with what you're doing. Also, you have to have patience, because not every day is the same and your level of interest is not always the same, and sometimes you're struggling with a text or something that is happening in meditation and it's easy to get discouraged. Patience is pretty much the prevalent attitude that you have to have.

Question: Can I ask you about cultivating this more sustained, more grounded happiness? I've noticed lately, actually, my underlying tone is generally pretty unhappy, even though I might often feel happy by certain conditions. I don't know if you have suggestions for cultivating that, for cultivating that sort of grounded, sustained, wholesome happiness.

Dharma Master Heng Chih: Probably, you would have to figure out some practices—such as recitation, bowing, or meditation—that can help you discover what's unhappy in there. What you will probably find is that the underlying tone comes from mistakes you made in the past, or attitudes that you have built up over time. Finding those might result in you having to repent for such things you've done, or find somebody you trust and whose intelligence you respect and talk to him or her about those things to get it off of your chest. Because as long as it is in there, it's going to be that base tone that sort of goes through your life.

So I think you have to delve deep, and some meditation can do it. You'll discover things in meditation. Repentance can do it.

Question: As human beings, we're deeply social. The yearning for love and recognition is deeply ingrained in our hearts. Often the people we are close to may end up hurting us in some way or at the very least sometimes we have to make decisions in life that people around us do not all support. A deep sense of loneliness comes from this. How can I deal with that? How can I find the strength to depend on myself?

Dharma Master Heng Chih: I think loneliness is a basic affliction. It's an affliction and it is not useful, but I think most of us experience it. We don't really know each other, I think, even at the deepest level. This is even true when the ties are so strong as between a mother and her son, for example. Whether it is with partners, friends, family, and so on —I think there's always parts of us that we keep or that we can't bring out. That's when we experience the loneliness.

I remember my teacher, Master Hsuan Hua, would talk to us early on when I was still a lay person working in San Francisco. He'd talk about loneliness, and that we had to find a way to let loneliness go. So, I can think of two ways that I do that.

One of them is in community. Here, in monastic life, there is some sort of camaraderie that goes on that's very supportive and I am sure you can also find community like that among the laity. If you can find people who have similar interests and similar beliefs and you can trust them, then you can work with your loneliness.

The other way is meditation. You could contemplate "Who's lonely?" It's self-centered: *Me, me, me. I'm lonely, nobody cares for me, nobody understands me* [*chuckles*], but it's not easy.

I think it's all-pervasive, everybody has it. So, I guess, positively you would look at what loneliness is and where it stems from by asking "Who's lonely?" and what does it mean and does it matter if we're lonely? We can still go on with life. I mean, you [*gestures to other student*] were just talking about an underlying unhappiness; you can still go on with life and when we're lonely we can still go on with life.

I've experienced a lot of loneliness as a monastic, because for many years I had no one from my culture to speak to, because I was sent out to the branches and the branches were all Asian people speaking Cantonese or Taiwanese or whatever—Aussie accents [*laughs*]. It was very hard to find somebody that I could communicate with. Even when you do communicate, it isn't bound to get out the loneliness. So, I guess we have to live with it. It is definitely something that is found in the Saha world[19] , and you can ask yourself, *Why did I come here? If I only had known that I was going to experience all of this?* You made the choice, so why did you come? Why did I come?

And if you came on vows, that's good—then you just deal with your loneliness. If you came 'resisting,' well that's another matter and you will have to own up. It was you who did it, it wasn't your parents, wasn't anybody else, you decided. [*A heavy sigh and laughter.*] You made your bed, now you lie in it.

Question: You mentioned that Master Hsuan Hua would comment on loneliness. What was the context when Master Hua spoke about loneliness?

Dharma Master Heng Chih: Well, we were brand new at that time at the Buddhist Lecture Hall. We

_____

19. Our world system is known as the Sahā World, a world in which people endure suffering.

were young Americans who were probably university-aged people or younger, and all of a sudden—especially those of us who were headed towards monasticism, but even others—right off the Śūraṅgama session (1968), a lot of lay people, probably forty or fifty people in the session coming and going, changed their jobs, sold their houses, changed their lives and came to San Francisco so they could listen to the *Lotus* and *Avataṃsaka Sūtra* lectures. And we were uprooted, I guess you could say.

So, he talked to us very gently during that time like a kind old father, and tried to encourage us. And it was lonely, because there were now no friends, no family for a lot of us. We were in a new town, new living situation, we knew each other but didn't really like each other [*laughs*]—that's how community is. You had to take pot luck. So it was in that context. He was very gentle, but at the same time he let us know that loneliness is ego-based, it's an affliction, it takes two to tango: if you don't want to be lonely, if you don't want to be stressed, you can figure out what to do.

Question: We know that you yourself were sick for a long time earlier this year. What type of practice do you find useful when you are sick?

Dharma Master Heng Chih: I only have one word for that: patience. [*Chuckles.*]

Because often you cannot do any practice—I was very sick; for two weeks I was only sleeping, not even eating for days. And then I began to come back. If you can meditate, that's good. If you can say the Buddha's name, or whatever your practice is, that's good. But sometimes the disease or the temporary illness is so severe you can't really do those things, so I think it's just a matter of patience. You shouldn't be too hard on yourself, and you should try to get yourself back up to where your energy was. My energy is now about back to 75%? It's come up a lot.

So, in long-term illness, it depends on a person's vigor and faith. We've seen people come and go, especially living here—they come and go. But, even when there's a lot of pain or there's not much energy, if you have faith then you can carry on. If you don't have the breath to say your practice out loud then you just say it in your mind, and often in the Tower of Blessings, where the elder nuns reside, we help each other. They helped me a lot when I was sick, physically helping me and mentally helping me get positive, when you really can't do it yourself.

I know that someone who's a real practitioner can be inspiring to others who watch him or her go through the process of terminal illness, who observe how a long-term cultivator deals with the process of dying. In such cases, I would again say the primary factor is patience.

The Teachers

Reverend Heng Sure

Reverend Heng Sure, Ph.D., ordained as a Buddhist monk in the Chinese Mahāyāna tradition at the City of Ten Thousand Buddhas, Talmage, California, in 1976. Born in Toledo, Ohio, he was finishing his M.A. in Oriental Languages at the University of California, Berkeley when he met his teacher, the late Chan Master Hsuan Hua (1916–1995). After his ordination, he commenced a "Three Steps, One Bow" pilgrimage dedicating his efforts to World Peace traveling up the California coast highway from South Pasadena to Ukiah, a distance of over six hundred miles in two years and nine months.

Rev. Sure regularly leads lectures, seminars, and retreats in a variety of venues on at least three continents a year. He is fluent in Mandarin, and also speaks French and some Japanese. He is involved in work on a new translation of the *Avataṃsaka Sūtra* and has recently completed a translation of the *Sixth Patriarch Sūtra* with Dr. Martin Verhoeven.

He has been an active participant in the interfaith community for many years and is also an accomplished musician and guitarist, translates traditional liturgical Buddhist music from Chinese and has written many Buddhist songs. He currently serves as Director of the Berkeley Buddhist Monastery, the Chair of the Dharma Realm Buddhist Association, and holds a Doctorate in Religion from the Graduate Theological Union, Berkeley, California.

Dharma Master Heng Lai

Dharma Master Heng Lai was ordained at the City of Ten Thousand Buddhas in 1976. Currently he is the Director of Snow Mountain Monastery in Index, Washington, where he leads regular recitation and meditation retreats. He also teaches throughout North America at Buddha Root Farm in Reedsport, Oregon, Gold Summit Monastery in Seattle, Washington, Avataṃsaka Monastery in Calgary, Alberta, and Gold Buddha Monastery in Vancouver, British Columbia.

Dharma Master Heng Lyu

Dharma Master Heng Lyu is the Abbot of the City of Ten Thousand Buddhas and the Vice-President of Dharma Realm Buddhist Association. The City of Ten Thousand Buddhas is a monastery and community that is home to a retreat center that offers retreats throughout the year, the Saṅghā Laity Training Program, Dharma Realm Buddhist University, Instilling Goodness and Developing Virtue K-12 private schools, and a volunteer program. He ordained as a Buddhist monk and was ordained at the City of Ten Thousand Buddhas in 1990.

Dharma Master Heng Chih

Dharma Master Heng Chih was one of the first Americans to be ordained in 1969 under the guidance of the Venerable Master Hsuan Hua, the founder of the City of Ten Thousand Buddhas. She is the only Western Mahāyāna Bhikshuni who currently holds the most precept years in the world.

She has been translating Buddhist texts such as the *Śūraṅgama Sūtra*, the *Vajrā Prajñā Pāramitā Sūtra*, and the *Avataṃsaka Sūtra* from Chinese to English for over 40 years. She has also taught extensively in the United States, Canada, Taiwan, and Australia. Currently, she serves as the Chair of the Board for Dharma Realm Buddhist University, and lectures and leads Dharma assemblies in North America, Australia, and Asia.

Martin Verhoeven

Martin Verhoeven, Ph.D., is currently Professor of Buddhist Classics at Dharma Realm Buddhist University, as well as Adjunct Professor of Comparative Religion at the Graduate Theological Union, in Berkeley. He also teaches a weekly translation and meditation series at the Berkeley Buddhist Monastery that is open to the community and broadcast online.

Dr. Verhoeven's background includes both academic study of history and various philosophical traditions and Buddhist practice. He was a Visiting Scholar at Stanford under a Ford Fellowship in the 1970s. In 1976, he met and trained under the Venerable Master Hsuan Hua, becoming a monk (with the name Heng Chau) in 1977, and took full ordination in 1979.

His study with Master Hua took him to monasteries around the world. It also led him to undertake a three-year, 800-mile bowing pilgrimage up the California coast with Reverend Heng Sure from 1977 to 1979. After 18 years as a monk, Dr. Verhoeven returned to lay life, but continued to study and teach Buddhism and related topics in the U.S. as well as in Asia, Europe, and Canada. He completed his Ph.D. at the University of Wisconsin-Madison on the American encounter with Asian religions. His particular areas of interest are the historical teachings of Buddhism, the Euro-American encounter with Asian religions, and the process of religious acculturation.

Douglas Powers

Douglas Powers took refuge with the Venerable Master Hsuan Hua at the World Peace gathering in Seattle in 1974. From 1980-1986, he was the Director of the Buddhist Council for Refugee Rescue and Resettlement. He taught students at Berkeley High School in the International Baccalaureate, Advanced Placement, and Honors programs for more than forty years.

He currently is a professor of Western Comparative Hermeneutics, Western Classics, and Buddhist Sūtras in both the undergraduate and graduate programs at Dharma Realm Buddhist University. He also serves as the Vice-President of Finance and Administration.

On Wednesday nights, Professor Powers teaches DRBU Extension course open to the public called "Buddhism for the Modern Mind", and leads the well-attended Guanyin retreats at the City of Ten Thousand Buddhas and summer retreats at Sudhana Center in Ukiah, CA and Buddha Root Farm in Reedsport, OR. He holds an M.A. from the Graduate Theological Union, and a M.A.T. and B.A. from the University of the Redlands.

Biographical Sketch of the Venerable Master Hsuan Hua

The Venerable Master Hsuan Hua (1918-1995), founder of the City of Ten Thousand Buddhas, was born into a poor family in a small village in Manchuria. He attended school for only two years before he had to return home to take care of his ailing mother. At home, he opened a free school for both children and adults who had even less opportunity than he did. Also as a young boy, he had his first encounter with death and became aware of the impermanence of life. Upon learning that Buddhism had a method for ending the cycle of death and rebirth, he resolved to become a monk.

Although his mother supported his aspirations for becoming a monk, she asked him to stay at home until she passed away. Master Hua, as a filial son, took care of her until her passing when he was nineteen. Thereupon he entered monastic life under Venerable Master Chang Zhi at Three Conditions

Monastery in Harbin. He then spent three years in solitary meditation beside his mother's grave.

Seeing firsthand the hungry and impoverished, he began to practice eating one meal a day, wishing that the food he did not eat would go to feed others. He also diligently studied the Buddhist scriptures, while maintaining a vigorous practice. He felt that both were needed to gain a balanced understanding of Buddhism. In 1948, he went to pay his respects to Chan Master Xuyun, who transmitted the Weiyang lineage of the Chan School to Master Hua.

In 1962, Master Hua came to the United States, and by 1968 he had established the Buddhist Lecture Hall in San Francisco, where he taught many young Americans. In 1969, five Americans resolved to become monastics and began the Buddhist monastic tradition in America. During the subsequent years, the Master trained and oversaw the ordination of hundreds of monks and nuns who came from all over the world to study with him.

Believing in the importance for Buddhists to ground themselves in the Buddha's teachings, Master Hua gave straightforward and practical commentaries on the sūtras. He founded the Buddhist Text Translation Society in order to translate these texts into the various languages of the world.

Master Hua also had a lifelong commitment to education. He established a number of schools and exhorted educators and students to think of school not only as a place to learn a skill but as a place to develop virtue and character. He considered every place a classroom and every moment was an opportunity to learn and grow.

With an open heart, the Master welcomed people of diverse religious faiths and backgrounds. He once asked the exiled Roman Catholic leader Paul Cardinal Yubin if he would be "a Buddhist among the Catholics," adding, "and I'll be a Catholic among the Buddhists. If we work together we can bring peace among our religions." Cardinal Yubin subsequently helped the Master found the Institute for World Religions. As a guest speaker at interfaith gatherings, the Master exhorted people to be true followers of their religious founder's vision and not fight amongst themselves.

Master Hua was a wonderful storyteller with a great sense of humor, a kind father figure who gave encouragement when times were hard, and a strict teacher who held his disciples to high standards. Throughout his life, he hoped to serve as a bridge for others to walk on, so that they could go from confusion and suffering to wisdom and happiness.

The Eight Guidelines of the Buddhist Text Translation Society

The Buddhist Text Translation Society (BTTS) is dedicated to making the Buddha's teachings available to Western readers in a form that can be directly applied to practice. In order to ensure that the translation process itself is done in the spirit of self-cultivation, Master Hua established Eight Guidelines for BTTS translators and volunteers.

1. A volunteer must free himself or herself from the motives of personal fame and profit.
2. A volunteer must cultivate a respectful and sincere attitude free from arrogance and conceit.
3. A volunteer must refrain from aggrandizing his or her work and denigrating that of others.
4. A volunteer must not establish himself or herself as the standard of correctness and suppress the work of others with his or her faultfinding.
5. A volunteer must take the Buddha-mind as his or her own mind.

6. A volunteer must use the wisdom of Dharma-Selecting Vision to determine true principles.
7. A volunteer must request Virtuous Elders in the ten directions to certify his or her translations.
8. A volunteer must endeavor to propagate the teachings by printing and distributing sūtras, *śāstras*, and *vinaya* texts when the translations are certified as being correct.

Resources

If the teachings in this booklet have inspired you, here are some further resources that may be of interest to you:

The **Berkeley Buddhist Monastery** (Berkeley, CA) aspires to provide a safe haven of tranquility and wisdom in an urban environment while carrying forward Master Hsuan Hua's (1918-1995) vision for education and interfaith harmony. A daily schedule of monastic practice combines with classes, lectures and cultural programs to make this monastery one of the more active spiritual centers of the Bay Area. www.berkeleymonastery.org/

The Buddhist Text Translation Society (BTTS) was founded in 1970 by the Venerable Master Hsuan Hua with the mission of translating the Chinese Buddhist Canon (Tripiṭaka) into English and other languages. To date, the Society has published over 200 volumes of Sūtra texts and instructional talks in English and Chinese, and also some texts in French, Italian, Spanish, and Vietnamese. BTTS also offers a selection of children's books and vegetarian cookbooks. www.buddhisttexts.org

The Dharma Realm Buddhist Association (DRBA) was founded by the Venerable Master Hsuan Hua in the United States of America in 1959. Taking the Dharma Realm as its scope, the Association aims make the Buddha's teachings available to the world in an authentic form. The DRBA website contains a variety of resources, including a list of its branch temples throughout North America and Asia, information on upcoming events, and links to further resources. www.drba.org

Dharma Realm Buddhist University (DRBU) is an educational community dedicated to liberal education in the broad Buddhist tradition—a tradition characterized by knowledge in the arts and sciences, self–cultivation, and the pursuit of wisdom. Its pedagogical aim is thus twofold: to convey knowledge and to activate an intrinsic wisdom possessed by all individuals. Developing this inherent capacity requires an orientation toward learning that is dialogical, interactive, probing, and deeply self-reflective. Such education makes one free in the deepest sense and opens the opportunity to pursue the highest goals of human existence. DRBU offers a four-year Bachelor of Arts in Liberal Arts with an emphasis on Eastern and Western Classical Texts, and a two-year Master of Arts in Buddhist Classics. www.drbu.org

DRBUx offers practitioners an opportunity to learn Dharma and put it into practice. Practitioners can attend workshops, retreats, as well as longer sessions to extend the scope of their practice in community. While serving others, practitioners open their hearts and engage the world. These are retreats where participants meditate in a Buddhist community, have a chance to find inner stillness, have fun, and bring the Dharma to life. www.drbux.org

Dedication of Merit

May the merit from this practice
Adorn all the Buddhas' Lands,
Repay the kindness from above
And rescue those in paths below.
May all who see or hear of this
Resolve upon Awakening,
And when this body meets its end,
Be born together in the Land of Bliss.

Dharma Realm Buddhist Association Monasteries

WORLD HEADQUARTERS
The City of Ten Thousand Buddhas
4951 Bodhi Way | Ukiah, CA 95482 U.S.A.
TEL: 707.462.0939 | FAX: 707.462.0949
www.drba.org

U.S.A.

CALIFORNIA

BERKELEY
Berkeley Buddhist Monastery
2304 McKinley Avenue
Berkeley, CA 94703 U.S.A.
TEL: 510.848.3440
www.berkeleymonastery.org

BURLINGAME
The International
Translation Institute
1777 Murchison Drive
Burlingame, CA 94010-4504
U.S.A.
TEL: 650.692.5912

LONG BEACH
Blessings, Prosperity, and
Longevity Monastery
4140 Long Beach Boulevard
Long Beach, CA 90807 U.S.A.
TEL/FAX: 562.595.4966

Long Beach Sagely Monastery
3361 East Ocean Boulevard
Long Beach, CA 90803   U.S.A.
TEL: (562) 438-8902

LOS ANGELES
Gold Wheel Monastery
235 North Avenue 58
Los Angeles, CA 90042   U.S.A.
TEL: 323.258.6668
FAX: 323.258.3619

SACRAMENTO
**The City of the
Dharma Realm**
1029 West Capitol Avenue
West Sacramento, CA 95691
U.S.A.
TEL: 916.374.8268
FAX: 916.374.8234

SAN FRANCISCO
Gold Mountain Monastery
800 Sacramento Street
San Francisco, CA 94108
U.S.A.
TEL: 415.421.6117
FAX: 415.788.6001

SAN JOSE
Gold Sage Monastery
11455 Clayton Road
San Jose, CA 95127 U.S.A.
TEL: 408.923.7243
FAX: 408.923.1064

MARYLAND

Avatamsaka Vihara
9601 Seven Locks RoadBethes-
da, MD 20817-9997 U.S.A.
TEL/FAX: 301.469.8300

WASHINGTON

INDEX
Snow Mountain Monastery
P.O. Box 272
50924 Index-Galena Road
Index, WA 98256   U.S.A.
TEL: 360.799.0699
FAX: 815.346.9141

SEATTLE
Gold Summit Monastery
233 1st Avenue
West Seattle, WA 98119   U.S.A.
TEL: 206.284.6690

CANADA

ALBERTA

Avatamsaka Monastery
1009 4th Avenue
s.w. Calgary, AB T2P OK8,
Canada
TEL: 403.234.0644

BRITISH COLUMBIA

Gold Buddha Monastery
248 East 11th Avenue
Vancouver, B.C. V5T 2C3,
Canada
TEL: 604.709.0248
FAX: 604.684.3754

AUSTRALIA

Gold Coast Dharma Realm
106 Bonogin Road
Bonogin, Queensland Au 4213
Australia
TEL: 61.755.228.788
FAX: 61.755.227.822

HONG KONG

Buddhist Lecture Hall
31 Wong Nei Chong Road,
Top Floor
Happy Valley, Hong Kong,
China
TEL: 852.2572.7644
FAX: 852.2572.2850

Cixing Chan Monastery
Lantou Island,
Man Cheung Po
Hong Kong, China
TEL: 852.2985.5159

MALAYSIA

**Dharma Realm Guanyin
Sagely Monastery**
161, Jalan Ampang
50450 Kuala Lumpur,
Malaysia
TEL: 03.2164.8055
FAX: 03.2163.7118

Prajna Guanyin
Sagely Monastery
Batu 51, Jalan Sungai Besi
Salak Selatan
57100 Kuala Lumpur, Malaysia
TEL: 03.7982.6560
FAX: 03.7980.1272

Fa Yuan Monastery
1 Jalan utama
Taman Serdang Raya
43300 Seri Kembangan
Selangor Darul Ehsan,
West Malaysia
TEL: 03.8948.5688

Malaysia DRBA
Penang Branch
32-32C, Jalan Tan Sri
Teh Ewe Lim
11600 Jelutong
Penang, Malaysia
TEL: 04.281.7728
FAX: 04.281.7798

Guan Yin Sagely Monastery
166A Jalan Temiang
70200 Seremban Negeri
Sembilan
West Malaysia
TEL/FAX: 06.761.1988

TAIWAN

Dharma Realm Buddhist
Books Distribution Society
11th Floor
85 Zhongxiao E. Road, Sec. 6
Taipei 115, Taiwan R.O.C.
TEL: 02.2786.3022
FAX: 02.2786.2674

Dharma Realm
Sagely Monastery
No. 20, Dongxi Shanzhuang
Liugui Dist.
Gaoxiong 844, Taiwan, R.O.C.
TEL: 07.689.3717
FAX: 07.689.3870

Amitabha Monastery
No. 136, Fuji Street,
Chinan Village, Shoufeng
Hualian County 974, Taiwan,
R.O.C.
TEL: 03.865.1956
FAX: 03.865.3426

SUBSIDIARY ORGANIZATIONS

Buddhist Text Translation Society
City of Ten
Thousand Buddhas
4951 Bodhi Way
Ukiah, CA 95482   U.S.A.
www.buddhisttexts.org
EMAIL: info@buddhisttexts.org
CATALOG: www.bttsonline.org

Dharma Realm Buddhist University
City of Ten
Thousand Buddhas
4951 Bodhi Way
Ukiah, CA 95482   U.S.A.
www.drbu.org

Dharma Realm Outreach
City of Ten
Thousand Buddhas
outreach@drba.org